Publishing

GN00336448

BRITTANY

BY
ELISABETH MORRIS

Produced by
Thomas Cook Publishing

Written by Elisabeth Morris
Original photography by Rick Strange

Edited and designed by Laburnum Technologies Pvt Ltd,
C-533 Triveni Apts, Sheikh Sarai Phase 1,
New Delhi 110017

Published by Thomas Cook Publishing
A division of Thomas Cook Holdings Ltd

PO Box 227, The Thomas Cook Business Park,
Units 19–21, Coningsby Road,
Peterborough PE3 8XX, United Kingdom
E-mail: books@thomascook.com
www.thomascookpublishing.com

ISBN: 1-841572-64-0

Head of Publishing: Donald Greig
Project Editor: Charlotte Christensen
Project Administrator: Michelle Warrington
DTP: Steven Collins

Series Consultant: Vivien Stone
Series Manager: Stephen York

Printed and bound in Spain by: Grafo Industrias Gráficas, Basauri.

Cover: Houses and turrets at Vitre.
Photograph by Michael Busselle/Robert Harding Picture Library.
Inside cover: photographs supplied by Spectrum Colour Library.

CD manufacturing services provided by business interactive ltd,
Rutland, UK.

Contents

Introduction

Jutting out into the Atlantic Ocean on the western edge of the European continent, Brittany is a part of France with unique appeal.

'The Bretons are born with seawater round the eyes, and the ocean flows through their veins.'

LOCAL PROVERB

You may have heard about Brittany from an enthusiastic friend or seen an enticing travel programme or brochure, and the name keeps turning up every time you think of holidays ahead. Colour shots flash through your mind: of rocks in a cloud of sea spray, of white sails on an emerald sea, of golden sand and gorgeous shellfish, of friendly quayside cafés. But you still ask yourself, 'Is it really for me? What kind of holiday can I expect?'

The key word is variety – and there is certainly enough of it in every sense.

The Two Faces of Brittany

The landscape of Brittany is literally defined by its contrasts. '*Armor*' (literally 'land of the sea') is the coastal fringe, its varied contours characterised by working harbours, seaside resorts, long stretches of wild, uninhabited shoreline, islands and cliffs teeming with birds. '*Argoat*' (the 'land of the woods') is green, inland Brittany, with its fields and forests, rivers, mountains, and moors.

The sea, the scudding clouds, and the omnipresent granite blend their greys and greens into a subtle yet powerfully attractive picture. Westerly winds – responsible for the changing moods of the sky – sweep vigorously over the land, ensuring summer temperatures that rarely soar.

The polders around Dol de Bretagne: the former marshlands are now cut with canals and farmed

B r i t t a n y

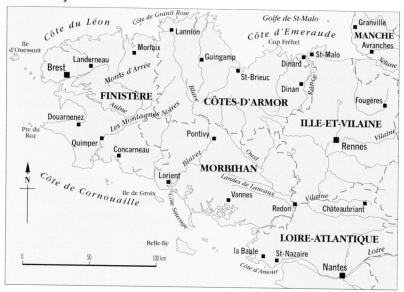

A Land of Traditions

The Bretons are a seafaring people with deep religious convictions. Megaliths, castles, parish closes, and calvaries are fascinating reminders that their culture is steeped in both paganism and Christianity. Their ancestral language, music, and costumes live on in the numerous festivals that take place in delightful old cities.

A Holidaymakers' Paradise

Whether you've an interest in fine food and drink, archaeology, fishing, church art, sunbathing, domestic architecture of the Middle Ages, birdwatching, castles, or canoeing – or in all of the above, and more – you'll find an opportunity in Brittany to pursue it.

You can drive through constantly changing scenery, walk through forests and across moors, cruise its rivers, and

cycle along canals. Relax on sheltered sandy beaches, sail round the islands, have a game of golf, or take the children to a water park.

Also included in this book are the lower reaches of the River Loire so as to include Nantes, the former capital of Brittany.

The Land

Covering an area of some 30,000sq km, the Breton peninsula has arrived at its present shape after æons of interaction between earth and elements. Its mountains were formed in the Primary Period. Around 600 million years ago, its granite was slowly eroded to its present height of less than 400m.

Pointe du Diable, Emerald Coast

A sudden rise in sea level during the Quaternary Period, which began a mere 2 million years ago, caused low-lying areas to be flooded: river valleys became *abers* (shallow estuaries), a distinctive feature of the jagged west coast, while hill tops became the numerous islands surrounding the peninsula.

Temperate Climate

With the warming influence of the Gulf Stream, winter is mild and temperatures stay above freezing, but storms can be spectacular in places such as the Pointe du Raz.

Spring is a busy time on the wildlife front, as the return of the warm weather brings intense activity in the numerous bird colonies, and the sudden blossoming of gorse all over the countryside.

In summer, temperatures average 18°C and, although the weather is sometimes unpredictable, the sun is never far away and shines generously on the beaches. Autumn lingers on peacefully inland, but the sea is starting to show signs of restlessness, heralding winter storms.

Granite boulders, near Le Castel

Abundant Nature

The constant struggle between sea and land has resulted in 2,500km of deeply indented coastline, with marked contrasts between the north, west, and south coasts. The ruggedness of the northern coastline is tempered by the unusual pink rock formations of the Côte de Granit Rose. To the west, taking the brunt of the onslaught of the mighty Atlantic, the coast of Finistère is austere, with dark sombre cliffs like those of the Crozon Peninsula. The sunny south coast stretches its long sandy beaches from le Pouldu to la Baule.

Tranquil waters wash the jagged teeth of the coastline off Point St-Mathieu

All round the coast, from Bréhat in the north to Belle-Ile in the south, the islands reflect the diversity of the mainland: large or small, fertile or barren, each has its own charm. Life along the coast is regulated by tidal movements which leave enormous areas uncovered and boats stranded. It is an absorbing pastime to gather shellfish at low tide, but it's wise to follow a timetable of the tides to avoid getting caught by rapidly rising waters.

Extending from the Ile d'Ouessant to the Montagnes d'Arrée, the Parc Naturel Régional d'Armorique creates a link between coastal and inland Brittany. Once entirely covered with dense forests, the undulating countryside offers a pleasing patchwork of fields separated by low stone walls, austere mountains, moors, rivers, and lakes.

Poor Land

Agriculture has always been important, although the land is generally poor – except along the coast, where the early vegetables of the Ceinture Dorée (Golden Belt) are grown in great quantities. Inland, apple orchards alternate with cornfields and pastures, with dairy produce and pork still forming a large proportion of agricultural production. The hard work needed to make a living on the land has forced countless generations of Bretons to rely on the wealth of the sea. Hence, farmers are often fishermen as well, although fishing is less lucrative than it used to be. The sea also provides a natural fertiliser in the form of *goémon*, a species of seaweed gathered at low tide.

Expanding Economy

Improved communications have pulled Brittany out of its long isolation, and decentralisation has given a boost to the region's economy. Poultry-farming is booming, and fish-farming and seaweed-farming also have a bright future. Although the food and car industries are doing well, the main fields of expansion are electronics, telecommunications, services, research, and tourism.

History

5000–2000 BC	Brittany's first known inhabitants, of obscure origin, erect the megaliths.
6th century BC	Arrival of the Celts. They call their new country Armor ('land by the sea'). Their society is well structured and they are skilled craftsmen and seafarers.
56 BC	The most powerful Celtic tribe, the Veneti from the region of Vannes, is defeated by Caesar in a sea battle off the Rhuys Peninsula.
56 BC–AD 350	The Roman occupation of Gallia Armorica brings peace, a new language (Latin), and a new religion (Christianity).
460	Massive immigration of more Celts from across the Channel, as they flee invading hordes of Angles and Saxons. They give Armorique a new name, Petite Bretagne (Little Britain), and rekindle the native population's religious fervour. The parish (*plou*) becomes the basic social and administrative unit throughout the country.

Jean de Montfort, Duke of Brittany

9th century	The Breton chief, Nominoë, becomes the first Duke of Brittany. In 845 Nominoë defeats his suzerain, the king of the Franks, and his son, Erispoë, becomes King of Brittany.
10th century	The Duke of Brittany, Alain Barbe-Torte ('Twisted Beard'), puts an end to Viking raids and chooses Nantes as his capital. After the death of Alain Barbe-Torte, the feudal lords defy the

authority of the Duke of Brittany, who is forced to acknowledge the King of France as his suzerain.

1341 The War of Succession begins, and the bitter conflict between France and England – both countries supporting contenders to the Duchy of Brittany – is brought to a head.

1364 The French contender, Charles de Blois, is defeated and killed at the Battle of Auray, which marks the end of the civil war. The English contender, Jean de Montfort, becomes Duke of Brittany.

1381 Jean de Montfort swears allegiance to the French King.

15th century The economic and cultural Golden Age of the Duchy of Brittany.

1488 Duke François II, leading a coalition against the French King, is defeated at the Battle of St-Aubin-du-Cormier and dies shortly afterwards, leaving the duchy to his 12-year-old daughter Anne.

1491 In order to end the conflict between France and Brittany, Anne marries the King of France, Charles VIII.

1499 After the death of Charles VIII, Anne marries the new King of France, Louis XII, who grants Brittany a certain amount of autonomy.

1514 Anne's daughter Claude marries the future King of France, François I, and gives him the Duchy of Brittany.

1532 After Claude's death, François I persuades the Breton parliament to ratify the Treaty of Union between France and Brittany, allowing the new province to keep some of its former independence.

1598 The Edict of Nantes, ending religious strife between Catholics and Protestants which has torn France apart since 1562, is signed by the King of France, Henri IV.

1660–1715 Reign of Louis XIV, the Sun King.

17th & 18th centuries	Relations between France and Brittany are often stormy, the main subject of quarrel being excessive taxation. In spite of this, the region's economy prospers.
14 July 1789	The Revolution starts in Paris with the storming of the dreaded Bastille.
1793–1804	The royalist Chouans lead Brittany into a guerilla-style war against the new French Republic. It ends with the execution of their chief, Georges Cadoudal.
19th century	The slow economic decline of Brittany prompts the birth of nationalist movements.
1940–45	The Breton people give wholehearted support to the Resistance movement. The postwar years are marked by an economic and cultural revival.
1962	First television link by satellite from Pleumeur-Bodou.
1966	Inauguration of the Rance estuary tidal power station.
1969	Small, disparate terrorist groups put forward demands for an independent Brittany.
1969–70	Creation of the Armorique and Brière Regional Nature Parks.
1975	The search for oil begins.
1977	Diwan schools (where lessons are taught in the Breton language) created.
1978	The oil tanker *Amoco Cadiz* sinks, sending oil slicks along the coast.
1985	Road signs throughout Britanny become bilingual (Breton/French).
1996	The Pope visits Brittany to take part in the pilgrimage of Ste Anne.
1999	The *Erika* sinks, bringing disastrous oil slicks to Brittany's coast.
2000	TV Breizh, the first all-Breton language TV station, is launched.
2000	The Brittany Revolutionary army is blamed for planting a bomb in a Prevert McDonalds which kills one member of the staff.
2001	Diwan schools are given full government grants.

The Breton flag reflects the region's identity

Governance

When the Act of Union was signed in 1532, Brittany became a French province, relinquishing all forms of autonomy and accepting policy decisions taken by the Government in Paris. Because this system proved detrimental to the region's economic development, the nationalist movement's popularity grew alongside general discontent until, in the 1980s, the regions were given increased economic responsibilities, which led to rapid modernisation. This policy is gradually showing positive results.

Central Government

France is a republic and Paris is the seat of government, comprising Parliament, the President, and the Government. Parliament consists of the National Assembly, elected for five years, which votes on the laws, and the Senate, elected for nine years, which proposes amendments.

The president of the Republic, elected for seven years, chooses the prime minister from the party that holds the majority in the National Assembly.

The president is chief of the armed forces and conducts foreign affairs jointly with the government, headed by the prime minister, assisted by a variable number of ministers. The government is answerable to the National Assembly.

There are several political parties, representing the whole spectrum of opinions from left to right.

Local Government

Brittany is administered by a Regional Council based in Rennes, which has the authority to take limited decisions in the fields of economic development, communications, education, and culture.

As in the rest of France, the region is divided into *départements*, each of which is run by a General Council that is based in the principal town (given in brackets).

The four *départements* of Brittany are: the Ille-et-Vilaine (Rennes), Côtes d'Armor (St-Brieuc), Finistère (Quimper), and Morbihan (Vannes).

The Breton Flag and the Triskell

The Breton flag was officially used for the first time in 1925, yet its symbolic meaning recalls Brittany's ancient history. The black and white stripes represent the nine original Breton bishoprics, while the ermine in the top left-hand corner is the heraldic symbol of the Duchy of Brittany.

The *triskell* is a decorative motif of Celtic origin found on ancient jewellery and coins throughout Europe and on Irish medieval manuscripts. Today, it is a symbol of Celtic identity.

The Celts

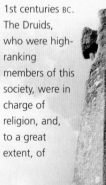

Brittany is today one of the last Celtic bastions of Western Europe. At a time when the making of Europe has focused public attention on cultural specificity, Brittany emerges as one of the cornerstones of European identity. Thus, the dream of a cultural awakening, nurtured by many Bretons since the 19th century, is being revived, and numerous associations and Celtic circles, encouraged by the Institut Culturel de Bretagne, do their utmost to preserve Brittany's Celtic heritage.

Gauls and Bretons

The Celtic invasions which took place around the 6th century BC are traditionally considered as having laid the foundations of the French nation, since they spread and prospered over the whole territory of what is now France and became known as Gauls. The desperate struggle of the Gauls against Caesar's legions is a subject of national pride from which has sprung the heroes of one of the most successful French cartoons – *Astérix*, translated into many languages. In the 5th century AD, Brittany received a second wave of Celts from across the Channel. Known as Bretons, they helped to reinforce the Celtic cultural impact on the whole region, which was both spiritual and material.

The Celtic Heritage

When they settled in Brittany, the Celts readily absorbed the civilisation of the megaliths which had preceded them, while theirs denoted a highly original combination of myth and reality.

Their well-structured society reached its peak during the La Tène period between the 5th and 1st centuries BC. The Druids, who were high-ranking members of this society, were in charge of religion, and, to a great extent, of

justice and education; poetic myths and legends played an important role in their teachings, and they conducted religious services in clearings in the forest. Human sacrifices were common practice.

Five powerful tribes occupied Brittany, including the Veneti in the south, whose ships boldly ventured on trading expeditions to the Mediterranean and to the British Isles.

But the Celts were above all farmers and clever craftsmen with a highly developed aesthetic sense, who shared a common language and artistic traditions with other Celtic countries, in particular Britain. Similarities in decoration have been found on ceramics on both sides of the Channel, for instance, the palm leaf of Greek origin; and on metal objects, a Celtic speciality, decorated with a great variety of original motifs and symbols such as the *triskell* (*see p11*). The Musée des Beaux Arts de Bretagne in Rennes and the Musée d'Archéologie Régionale in Nantes both have interesting collections of regional Celtic art.

Facing page above: Ist-century AD bronze head; below: Croas-Men, Lampaul-Ploudalmézeau
Above: a celebration of Brittany's Celtic heritage

Culture

The strength and specificity of Breton culture lies in the people's awareness of their past and in their will to maintain continuity, while accepting the challenge of changing economic and social conditions. This apparent contradiction stems both from the Breton temperament and from Brittany's geographical and historical context.

Curving lace *coiffes* follow each region's style

The highly individualistic and proud Bretons lived for centuries in voluntary isolation until well after Brittany was officially united with France. Later on, centralised economic policies and an inadequate communications network continued to keep Brittany in relative isolation until after World War II.

This context was detrimental to the economic life of the region, but at the same time it ensured the survival of the Celtic language and of a wealth of traditions, which today still form part of the Breton way of life. The sense of isolation also encouraged a highly original form of religious art to flourish.

Daily Life

To an outsider, daily life in Brittany appears very much the same as in any other region of France,

and, unless you arrive on the day a *pardon* or folk festival is taking place, you might well wonder what is so special about Brittany.

The same contrast exists between town and country as anywhere in France: two-thirds of the population now live in towns, and the number of jobs available in commerce, administration, and the services has tripled since the 1950s, a familiar trend throughout the country. Town centres are lively, with colourful markets, elegant shops, and enticing restaurants, while the countryside is deeply marked by traditional farming activities, still archaic in places.

The sea, however, is an element of daily life more omnipresent in Brittany than in other French regions: it epitomises the Breton spirit of independence, and, to

THOMAS COOK'S BRITTANY

Thomas Cook introduced excursions to Brittany as early as 1865. However, they aroused little interest until the 1880s; this was ascribed to the lack of a railway network, which was late to develop in the region.

This situation lingered, and even a decade later, Cook's own guidebook to the area mentioned (ironically as an advantage) the continuing scarcity of British visitors to the region.

By the turn of the century, however, tours of Brittany had caught on. Dinard, in particular, had become a highly popular favourite with Cook's customers.

many youngsters, going to sea is still an obsession.

The Bretons are, of course, very much a part of the French nation (although some nationalist extremists might disagree), and they bear certain characteristics, such as an individualistic temperament or a sense of hospitality, which foreigners promptly recognise.

But there are subtle differences between French people from various regions. The Bretons, for instance, are known for their changing moods: they can sometimes be uncommunicative and at other times enthusiastic; they also have a vivid imagination and a definite inclination towards fantastic stories and the supernatural.

Traditions

Having always felt the need to assert their cultural identity, the Bretons have jealously guarded their traditions which are today kept alive through folk festivals and colourful pageants steeped in Celtic culture, in which music, dance, and costumes are the essential ingredients, together with sporting contests and traditional games similar to those practised in other Celtic regions such as Cornwall and Scotland. Still very prominent in Breton life, religion also has its typical celebrations called *pardons*, which attract mixed crowds of believers and tourists (*see pp158–9*).

Costumes and Coiffes

The best celebrations are marked by special clothing, and folk festivals and *pardons* are no exception. The amazing variety of traditional dress is due to the fact that, in the past, each parish had its distinctive costume and lacy headdress (*coiffe*) which female parishioners wore for Mass on Sunday, for family gatherings, and for collective festive occasions. Nowadays, apart from festivals, *coiffes* are rarely seen except on some older women on Sundays.

The best-known costumes are from Cornouaille, where traditions have their strongest adherents. The main components of women's costumes are dresses, often black but richly embroidered; aprons covering the greater part of the dress fronts and elaborately decorated with lace and embroidered motifs; and, above all, *coiffes*, delicate like butterfly wings in Pont-Aven or rigid and rising high above the head in Bigouden country.

Men's costumes include embroidered waistcoats, short black jackets, and large-brimmed felt hats with a shiny buckle and long ribbons floating in the breeze.

Local Breton costumes, a treasured tradition, are worn with pride on high days and holidays

A satisfying camaraderie characterises the life of these fishermen at Dahouët port, le Val André

The Breton Language
Breton is still widely spoken, particularly in the western part of the region known as the Basse Bretagne. Closely related to Welsh, it is the only Celtic language spoken on the European mainland, and today it is taught in schools and at universities, while great efforts are made to promote its use among the native population through literature, radio broadcasts and television programmes.

Breton Arts and Crafts
Breton art found its most original expression in village churches and parish closes (see pp98–101) which bear witness to the religious fervour, bold imagination and artistic sense of the Breton people. There is a wealth of *musées des arts et traditions populaires* (crafts and traditions museums) where it is possible to admire Quimper pottery, delicate lace, and carved oak furniture, and, in particular, *lits clos*, beds enclosed within elaborately decorated cupboards as a protection against the cold.

Saints and Legends
To the Bretons, the world of the supernatural is an essential ingredient of their life, a metaphysical necessity. Out of this land of mists and marshes, forbidding sea and rugged hills, have come tales of dragons and demons, drowned cities and seductresses, giants and human sacrifice, fairies and men of faith. Incongruously, sacred and profane beliefs have actually nurtured one another down the ages, often to the dismay of Church authorities. If there are no saints without legends, it is also true to say that there are few legends without saints.

Little and Large
Congenial, sometimes naïve, and often good Christians, giants such as Hok-Bras and Gargantua erected megaliths and even created 'mountains' such as the Montagnes d'Arrée. Ogres and elves lurk in suspended animation in the remnants of once mighty forests such as Paimpont.

One charming legend tells how fairies, expelled from the Forest of Brocéliande, shed so many tears that the Golfe du Morbihan was formed. They threw into it their crowns of flowers, which changed into 365 islands, and three of them drifted out to sea – Houat, Hoëdic, and Belle-Ile, the loveliest of the three.

Breton fairies are helped by shy little beings called *korrigans*. There are sirens too, eternal temptresses as immortalised in Homer's *Odyssey*.

Heroes
The most famous of heroes is undoubtedly King Arthur, the central

character of a romantic cycle of legends in which religion and magic are in perfect harmony and Christian morality is upheld by all – including Merlin the magician. Arthur and his gallant friends were adopted into Breton folklore thanks to Celtic immigrants from Britain, and Arthurian legends are considered by the Bretons to have been based here rather than in Britain.

Sainted Men and Women

Local saints are considered family friends, and credited with healing powers against all kinds of diseases. Even animals have their own saint to protect them: thus, St Cornély is the patron saint of cattle.

Of the region's important saints, first of all there is St Anne, mother of Mary and patron saint of Brittany. According to legend, she was born in Brittany, went to Judea, married Joachim, gave birth to Mary, and later returned to her native country.

Jesus is said to have brought St Peter here to see his grandmother.

St Yves is another native, the most popular saint in Brittany. He is patron saint of lawyers and protector of the poor, a combination of interests that confounds modern cynicism.

Beside Fouesnant's church is a war memorial showing a peasant wearing the local headdress

F e s t i v a l s

The names of festivals remind us that most of them are rooted in the basic realities that used to characterise daily life in the past, celebrated because they were the very things that provided people with their livelihood: horses, cider, buckwheat, and above all, the sea, a theme that recurs again and again. These festivals overflow with music and dance, competitions, Celtic games, and a selection of gastronomic delights.

La Fete des Mouettes, Saint Bric sur Mer

Festou-noz (night feasts) are less sophisticated than folk festivals. Once they used to celebrate the completion of rural tasks such as the harvest. Today these local feasts still exist as occasions for people to drink and be merry as in earlier times. The most important festivals take place in Quimper, Lorient, Concarneau and Plozévet.

Festival de Cornouaille takes place in Quimper during the third week of July at the heart of the old town; and 4,000 participants, in various shows, offer music, singing, dancing, fairy tales, Breton games and exhibitions. *Tel: 02 98 55 53 53.*

Festival Interceltique is the major event of southern Brittany, in Lorient during August, with artists gathering from various Celtic countries. All the arts are represented; performances take place on stage and also in the streets. *Tel: 02 97 21 24 29.*

Grande Fête Folklorique des Filets Bleus, held in August in Concarneau, is named after the fishing nets traditionally used to catch sardines. *Tel: 02 98 50 88 81.*

Mondial'Folk de Plozévet in the small town of Plozévet in Finistère in July draws some 800 dancers, singers, and musicians

Traditions live on in the young

Embroidery, a speciality of Pont l'Abbé, lavishly covers costumes seen on special occasions

from 14 countries, including the best Breton groups. *Tel: 02 98 81 44 45.*

Below is a selection of summer folk festivals and traditional feasts.

July
Auray: Festival International d'Auray (international folk music), with stage and street performances.
Tel: 02 97 24 09 75.
Fougères: Voix des pays (a variety of performances). *Tel: 02 99 94 12 20.*
Fouesnant: Fête des Pommiers (Apple Tree Festival). *Tel: 02 98 56 00 93.*
Gourin: Grande Fête de la Crêpe (Pancake Festival).
Tel: 02 97 23 66 33.
Pont-l'Abbé: Fête des Brodeuses (Lace-makers' Festival).
Tel: 02 98 82 37 99.

August
Douarnenez: Festival International de Folklore (Folk Festival).
Tel: 02 98 92 13 35.
Guerlesquin: Marché Animé (street performances, every Monday).
Tel: 02 98 72 84 20.
Guingamp: Fête de la St-Loup: dancing, singing, Breton games and *festou-noz.*
Tel: 02 96 43 73 89.
Le Croisic: Fête de la Mer (Sea Festival).
Tel: 02 40 23 00 70.
Lamballe: Festival Folklorique des Ajoncs d'or (Folk Festival).
Tel: 02 96 31 05 38.
Roscoff: Fête de la Mer (Sea Festival).
Tel: 02 98 61 12 13.
St-Briac: Fête des Mouettes (Seagull Festival). *Tel: 02 99 88 07 67.*
Vannes: Fêtes d'Arvor, traditional music and dancing. *Tel: 02 97 47 24 34.*

Impressions

The sea is Brittany's greatest attraction: its changing moods are legendary, the views breathtaking, and the air invigorating, while the dense forests, wild moors and solitary mountains are shrouded in mystery, and the clear rivers abound in fish.

Benodet beach

In Brittany you can have a holiday that is tailor-made for you: you can be active or relax totally, join the holiday crowds or be completely on your own. You can stay in a lively seaside resort and come back with your hair full of sand, or you can spend a week roaming the countryside in a horse-drawn caravan.

You can enjoy the sophisticated life of Dinard or la Baule, book a room in a castle or stay on a farm. You can cut yourself off from civilisation on one of the fascinating islands, join a keep-fit course in a *thalassothérapie* centre, explore on horseback Brittany's most secluded areas or gallop along the cliff tops and on the beaches at low tide . . . the choice is yours.

FRANCE

(50) 🏘

(90) 🚗

(130) 🏛

Speed limits in sign language at the port of Roscoff

When to Go
The best time to visit Brittany is in late spring and summer, when the sun shines generously but a sea breeze keeps temperatures around 20°C. However, the weather can suddenly turn cool and showery. So come prepared and don't forget to bring a cardigan, a raincoat, and a pair of comfortable walking shoes, as well as beach clothes and sandals; you will probably use them all in the space of a single day!

If you like photography, a 200 ASA film will be perfectly suited to Brittany's capricious light.

Arriving
If you've arrived directly from abroad, don't forget that Brittany is part of France; the pavement cafés, the shops, the food stalls, and a quick glance at a restaurant menu will clear any doubt in your mind straight away. But, whatever you have heard about the Bretons' spirit of independence, remember that they are often as proud of being French as they are of being Bretons!

Lifestyle
Meal times are fairly rigid and restaurants may not serve you if you arrive too late; lunch is generally served from noon to 1.30pm and dinner from 7pm to 10pm.

As everywhere in France, meals are meant to be enjoyed, not rushed through, and you will find that many places, including sights, castles, museums and shops, are usually closed between noon and 2pm, making a definite lull in the day's activities which you will soon learn to appreciate and savour. To compensate for this interruption, shops usually extend their opening hours in the evening during the holiday season, but banks and museums do not.

The end of the season comes rather abruptly during the second half of September, and by the end of the month many sights are closed until the next spring, or sometimes only open at weekends.

Dress is informal except in certain hotels and casinos. Avoid beach clothes inside churches, which are crowded on Sunday mornings and should not be visited then for sightseeing.

People greet each other by shaking hands. They will appreciate your trying to speak French and will then come to your rescue in English if they can.

Local tourist offices will help with information and useful tips.

Opening Times

It is impossible to generalise about church opening times; in theory, churches are open during daytime, but in practice, they are often closed for fear of damage. Sometimes a notice on the door indicates where the key can be obtained, but this is not always the case and you must be prepared for some frustrating experiences when visiting churches.

For information, contact the local tourist offices.

Prettily patterned half-timbered façades above shops in Brittany's capital, Rennes

Getting Around

Maps

It is important to have a fairly detailed regional map that shows secondary roads and small villages, since prehistoric sites, castles, chapels, churches, and open-air museums are often well hidden in the heart of the countryside. The best maps are published by Michelin and the Institut

A road sign for British visitors

Géographique National. They are both reasonably priced and available in bookshops, hypermarkets, and through newsagents.

The more comprehensive Michelin map number 230 (1/200,000) is particularly suitable for visitors with cars, as the clearly graded roads make route-planning that much easier. The IGN map number 105 (1/250,000), on the other hand, is less detailed, but gives a better overall view of the region, and includes seven town plans.

Driving

Brittany is ideal touring country. Once you've arrived – and provided you keep away from the main seaside resorts – you'll find lots of quiet roads winding through the countryside, with delightful surprises in store for you whether or not you've planned your route in advance. Excursions can be based on various themes. Some of them, such as 'In the Painters' Footsteps' (*see pp112–13*) or 'Castles of Southern Brittany' (*see pp138–9*), are dealt with in this guide, but

there are many other possibilities that can be explained by local tourist offices.

Town centres are crowded, and their narrow streets often unsuitable for traffic. To avoid unnecessary delays, leave your car in one of the official car parks (remember to display a ticket where appropriate).

Cycling

Cycling in Brittany can be very enjoyable along the coast and inland except in mountainous areas. Cycle and mountain-bike trips, including accommodation for two to seven nights, are organised by Loisirs Accueil, a service provided by the Comité Départemental du Tourisme in Rennes, St-Brieuc and Vannes.

Walking

Walking in Brittany is particularly rewarding and gives an exhilarating feeling of freedom. There is a wide choice of guided and self-guided hiking tours, again organised by Loisirs Accueil, from a weekend along the Côte de Granit Rose to a two-week hike across Brittany from the Golfe du Morbihan on the south coast to Lannion on the north coast. Loisirs Accueil in Brittany now centres around Loisirs Accuiel Côtes d'Armor Tourisme (*tel 02 96 62 72 15; fax 02 96 62 72 25; www.cotesdarmor.com*).

Sailing and Cruising

Sailing trips are available all along the coast for beginners and experienced sailors alike, and are a good way to discover Brittany's coastline (information available from tourist offices).

Where to Go

The Breton peninsula can be divided into four main areas. To the east are Rennes and the so-called border areas, which used to mark the frontier between France and Brittany and which have a wealth of magnificent defensive castles. It is an area of rolling hills, beautiful woodland, and wandering rivers, with the regional capital, Rennes, in its centre.

Facing the coast of Cornwall across the English Channel, northern Brittany has long forgotten the days of privateering and long-distance fishing. Today, the varied coastline, in turn rugged and tame, is lined with fashionable resorts and the historic town of St-Malo. The sunny coast of southern Brittany is edged with long golden beaches and a vast natural reserve, the Golfe du Morbihan. The countryside is mellow, with river valleys and peaceful old towns. Situated at the head of the busy Loire estuary, Nantes is the region's largest conurbation.

Surrounded by the sea on three sides, Finistère is the most authentically Breton of the four areas, with typical coastal activities, a firmly established agricultural economy, and a culture deeply attached to its traditions.

Seaside resorts have great charm, while the Montagnes d'Arrée and Montagnes Noires are extremely rich scenically and culturally. At the heart of Cornouaille, Quimper is one of the most attractive towns in Brittany.

Walking along the cliff path of Cap Sizun to the Enfer de Plogoff

Where to Find . . .

Far from being exhaustive, the list given below is only a thematically-arranged selection of the best sites, monuments, etc.

Abbeys: Landévennec (Crozon Peninsula), St-Gildas-de-Rhuys.

Beaches: Dinard, St-Lunaire, St-Cast-le-Guildo, le Val-André, Trégastel-Plage (north coast); Bénodet, Mousterlin, Beg Meil, and Cap Coz (south Finistère); Quiberon, la Trinité-sur-Mer, la Baule (south coast).

Bird reserves: Les Sept Iles (off the Côte de Granit Rose), Golfe du Morbihan (south coast).

Calvaries: Plougastel-Daoulas and Tronoën (Finistère); Guéhenno (Morbihan, north of Vannes).

Castles: Combourg, Montmuran (north of Rennes), les Rochers-Sévigné (east of Rennes), Fougères, Vitré, Fort la Latte (west of Dinard), la Roche-Jagu (near Tréguier), Kerjean (south of Roscoff), Josselin (near Ploërmel), Suscinio (Rhuys Peninsula), Nantes.

Churches: Quimper, Tréguier and Dol cathedrals, Saint-Sauveur (Dinan), Kreisker Chapel (St-Pol-de-Léon), Runan (north of Guingamp), St-Herbot (south of Morlaix), Pont-Croix (southwest of Douarnenez), Loctudy (south Finistère), Ste-Barbe (north of Quimperlé), Ste-Noyale (northeast of Pontivy).

Church interiors: Lamballe, Loc-Envel (west of Guingamp), Notre-Dame-du-Tertre (Châteaudren, *see p147*),

All set for serious relaxation at Dinard

Kerfons (south of Lannion), Lampaul-Guimiliau (south of Morlaix), St-Fiacre, Kernascléden (north of Quimperlé).

Cliffs: Cap Fréhel (north coast), Crozon Peninsula, Pointe du Raz (Finistère).

Domestic architecture: Granite – Locronan (north of Quimper), Rochefort-en-Terre (east of Vannes). Timber-framed – Quimper, Morlaix, Rennes, Dol-de-Bretagne.

Fishing rivers: Léguer and Trieux (north coast, salmon, and trout), Aulne (Finistère, salmon), Scorff (trout), and Blavet (south coast, salmon).

Forests: Paimpont (west of Rennes), Huelgoat (Finistère), Quénécan (Guerlédan Lake).

Islands: Bréhat (north coast), Ouessant and Sein (Finistère), Belle-Ile (south coast).

Lakes: Guerlédan (north of Pontivy).

Megaliths: la Roche-aux-Fées (south of Rennes), Barnenez (north of Morlaix), Lagatjar (Crozon Peninsula), Carnac and Locmariaquer (south coast).

Oyster beds: Cancale (north coast), Etel and Pénerf rivers (south coast).

Parish closes: St-Thégonnec, Guimiliau, Pleyben (Finistère).

Parks and gardens: Caradeuc (north-west of Rennes), les Rochers-Sévigné, Kerguéhennec (west of Ploërmel).

Walled cities: St-Malo, Dinan, Concarneau, Vannes, Guérande.

A shopping street in Vannes

Rennes and the East

The eastern part of Brittany, which has Rennes as its main town, is the least influenced by the sea, but is Breton all the same. The limits of this 'border area' adjoining the rest of France are roughly those of the Ille-et-Vilaine *département* (its small section of coastline, which belongs to the Côte d'Emeraude, is dealt with under Northern Brittany).

Fougrès on the Nançon

Rural Image

Named after the two main rivers that flow through it and meet in Rennes, the Ille-et-Vilaine is in many ways a transition area. Its rolling hills and rich pastures, hemmed in by tall hedges and alternating with wide-open fields, are not unlike those of Normandy, its close neighbour to the northeast, while its lazy rivers winding their way through the countryside are reminiscent of the Loire region to the south.

However, the woodland areas are unmistakably Breton, and still evoke the mystery of Celtic legends. The Paimpont Forest of today is but a remnant of the dense Brocéliande, one of ancient Europe's finest hunting forests which once cloaked most of inland Brittany. Where else but here could you expect to see the fountain where Merlin the Magician first met the beautiful Viviane?

Difficult Dual Role

The Rennes region still bears evidence of the double role it played throughout its troubled history as the gateway to Brittany and the first line of defence against intruders from the east. All the ambiguity of this dual function is contained in the expression used by the well-loved Duchess Anne who, when referring to the mighty fortress of Fougères, called it 'the key to my treasure'. But did she intend to use that key to lock up her treasure or, on the contrary, to unlock the door and let visitors in? Much later the area was again at the heart of political strife when, during the French Revolution, there was fierce fighting between French troops and Breton royalists trying to keep them out of Brittany.

Cultural Melting Pot

By virtue of its location, the region has always been more open to outside influences than the rest of Brittany. As early as the Middle Ages, pilgrims on their way to Santiago de Compostela in Spain went right through it, traditionally stopping at Dol-de-Bretagne in the north and Redon in the south.

The French language was adopted more readily in Ille-et-Vilaine than in Basse (Lower) Bretagne, and today few people speak Breton here, although it is taught at Rennes University.

Moreover, every year, when Rennes and its region stage splendid festivals, some of the best and most colourful Breton traditions are displayed side by side with those from other regions of Brittany. Considerable economic development and improved communications in Rennes in the last 30 years have enhanced the region's role as the gateway to Brittany.

Rennes and the East

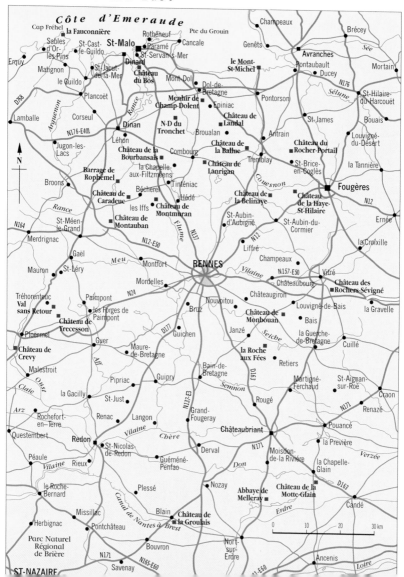

Rennes

Rennes was founded by the Celts 2,000 years ago at the centre of a rich agricultural basin where the Ille and Vilaine rivers meet. When Brittany became a duchy, both Rennes and Nantes claimed the title of capital, and the struggle for supremacy went on for centuries.

Enjoying a cup of coffee in old Rennes

After the signing of the Treaty of Union between France and Brittany in 1532, the city became the seat of the Breton Parliament and the region's cultural and administrative centre. Marking its new status, elegant stone buildings were erected next to the timber-framed houses. But the centre was destroyed by fire in 1720 and rebuilt shortly afterwards in French classical style with broad open spaces.

During the 19th century, the town spread south of the Vilaine and the university was founded. The designation of Rennes as the capital of Brittany in 1956 put an end to centuries of rivalry with Nantes and marked the beginning of the city's economic revival. Improved communications gave Rennes a chance to invest in high technology and develop traditional industries such as the car industry (Citroën), the food industry, and publishing (*Ouest-France* is France's biggest daily newspaper).

Rennes' population has already exceeded the 210,000 mark and the town is still expanding, while preserving its historic centre situated on the right

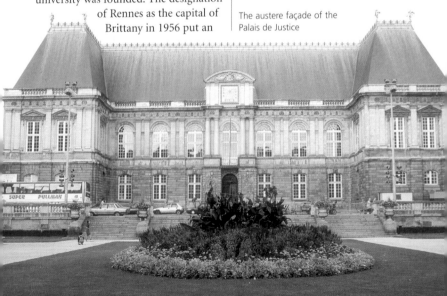

The austere façade of the Palais de Justice

R e n n e s

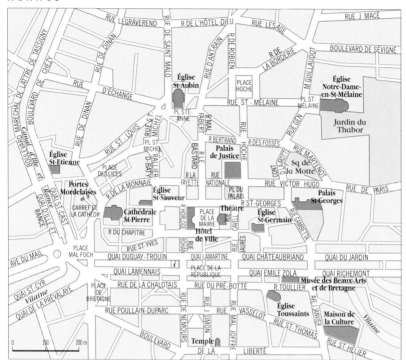

bank of the Vilaine. This can be divided into two distinct parts: old Rennes and the adjoining 18th-century town.

Old Rennes

This is essentially located round the cathedral. The Portes Mordelaises nearby is all that remains of the town walls.

Cathédrale St-Pierre

The two towers are the only remaining parts of the original building dating from the 16th and 17th centuries, since the cathedral was rebuilt at the end of the 18th century and the interior richly decorated. Note the 16th-century Flemish altarpiece.

Carrefour de la Cathédrale.
Open: 8.30am–noon & 2–5pm.

Medieval Streets

Behind the cathedral, several narrow streets have medieval and Renaissance half-timbered houses, some of them corbelled, with beautifully carved beams. The most picturesque streets are

Rennes is situated 347km southwest of Paris on the A11 motorway and 71km south of the Channel port of St-Malo, which has regular ferry crossings from Portsmouth, Poole, Jersey, and Guernsey. It is two hours from Paris by TGV (fast train). Direct flights to Rennes/St-Jacques Airport from Paris, London, and most large French towns.

The Thabor Gardens, a pleasure in any season

the rue St-Yves, rue du Chapitre, rue de la Psalette, and rue St-Guillaume, where you can admire the remarkable 16th-century house known as Du Guesclin's House. At the end of the rue du Chapitre, on the edge of the medieval quarter, the imposing 18th-century Hôtel de Blossac offers a marked contrast with the neighbouring houses.

North of the cathedral, the long place des Lices, which was once used for tournaments in medieval times, is surrounded by several 17th-century residences built for members of the Breton parliament. The old town extends further north along the rue St-Michel to the place Ste-Anne.

Palais de Justice

This magnificent edifice marks the transition between the old town and the 18th-century town. It was built between 1618 and 1655 by Salomon de Brosse, the architect of the Luxembourg Palace in Paris, to house the Breton parliament. Austere outside, it is lavishly decorated inside with gilt carved wood panelling,

coffered ceilings and paintings. The Grande-Chambre is the most remarkable hall in the palace. When the architect Gabriel rebuilt Rennes in the 18th century, he slightly altered the façade. In 1994, the palace was devastated by a fire, but has now been restored to its full glory.
Place du Palais. Tel: 02 99 67 11 11. Guided tours available.

The 18th-Century Town

The principal architect of the 'new' town was Gabriel, who designed the place de la Concorde in Paris. Its centre is the vast place de la Mairie, with the Town Hall and the theatre at either end.

Église Notre-Dame-en-St-Melaine and Jardin du Thabor

St-Melaine, to the east of the town centre, is a former abbey church. The tower and the intersection between the nave and the transept date from the 11th century. Inside, a 15th-century fresco depicts Christ's baptism. On the north side are the 17th-century cloisters.

The Thabor Gardens, in the abbey grounds, were a favourite haunt of Romantic writer Chateaubriand (*see p50*), and include a formal French garden, a rose garden, and an English-style park.
Place St-Melaine. Church open: 8.30am–7pm. Gardens open: times vary with the seasons.

Hôtel de Ville (Town Hall)

The Town Hall was built in Louis XV style between 1734 and 1743. At the centre of the elegant curved façade stands an imposing belfry; below the

pediment, an empty recess originally contained a bronze statue of Louis XV, destroyed during the Revolution. In the left wing, 18th-century tapestries from Brussels hang over the staircase, and the Great Hall is decorated with symbols of Breton cities. Facing the Town Hall across the square, the theatre (open for performances) was built in 1832.
Place de la Mairie. Tel: 02 99 28 55 55. Open: weekdays 9am–5pm, guided tours. Admission charge.

Musée des Beaux-Arts and Musée de Bretagne

Both are situated on the south bank of the river, in a former university building dating from the 19th century. The Musée des Beaux-Arts contains an important collection of paintings from the 14th to the 20th-centuries, with masterpieces such as *Perseus and Andromeda* by Veronese, *Tête de Femme* by Picasso, and works by Corot, Boudin, Sisley, Gauguin and the School of Pont-Aven. The jewel of the collection is the *Nouveau-Né* by the 17th-century French painter Georges de la Tour, a moving study of two women watching over a new-born baby.

The Musée de Bretagne is a regional museum illustrating Brittany's history

through various objects, documents, sculptures, jewellery, and handicrafts. There are six sections: Prehistory, Gallo-Roman Armorique, the Middle Ages, the Ancien Régime (1532–1789), the 19th century, and Brittany Today.
20 quai Emile-Zola. Tel: 02 99 28 55 85 (Beaux Arts); 02 99 28 55 84 (Bretagne). Open: 10am–noon & 2–6pm. Closed: Tue. Admission charge.

Nearby
Ecomusée du Pays de Rennes

This open-air museum, 8km south of Rennes, illustrates the history of farming from the 16th century onwards.
Route de Châtillon-sur-Seiche, 35200 Rennes. Tel: 02 99 51 38 15. Open: 2– 6pm. Closed: Mon. Admission charge.

Parc Ornithologique de Bretagne

Located at Bruz, 12km south of Rennes, the park has a fascinating collection of more than a thousand exotic birds.
53 boulevard Pasteur, 35170 Bruz. Tel: 02 99 52 68 57. Open: daily, Jul–Aug 10am–noon & 2–7pm; Sep–Jun 10am–noon & 2–6pm. Admission charge.

The grand Town Hall, in the classical quarter

Touring Brittany, you can spot a castle round almost every bend of the road. Some hide behind a screen of foliage, others open their gates to offer a close-up view of their exterior. A few can be visited, and it is a thrilling experience to wander through bare, chill rooms or tastefully furnished halls and libraries full of leather-bound volumes. For these dwellings of bygone days hold within their walls evidence of the lives of their often forgotten occupants.

Some 4,000 castles in Brittany reflect the changing lifestyle and the economic ups and and downs of a society through 10 centuries of war and peace. Changes in architectural styles were prompted not only by necessity but also by fashion, for in spite of Brittany's prolonged isolation, main artistic trends flourishing in France and Italy influenced master builders and landowners, who brought back new ideas from their extensive travels. Thus, Madame de Sévigné introduced the comfort and elegance of the French court in her beloved castle of les Rochers-Sévigné near Vitré.

Whatever their style, Brittany's castles all bear an undeniable stamp of authenticity: the granite with which they were built – often with contrasting white sandstone – from the 17th century onwards.

Defensive Fortresses

Defensive fortresses were erected by feudal lords in strategic places – on a river bank, like Josselin in

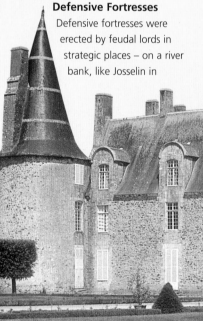

Morbihan, or on a promontory facing the sea, like Fort la Latte near Cap Fréhel. Some castles were built by the Dukes of Brittany or came into their possession, and a fortified town grew up round them, as in Dinan and Fougères.

Splendid Residences

Once the threat of war had abated, castles became a symbol of prosperity and of political power. Many, like Caradeuc near Bécherel and la Bourbansais south of Dinan, were built by influential members of the Breton parliament during the 17th and 18th centuries. At the end of the 19th century, an exaggerated taste for grandeur led to the building of such follies as Trévarez at the heart of the Montagnes Noires. At the same time a great variety of more modest edifices mushroomed all over the countryside. These manor houses were the homes of the less affluent Breton nobility or the country houses of rich ship owners, usually based in St-Malo. Two of the best examples are the Château du Bos, south of St-Malo, and the Manoir de Kérazan, near Loctudy in south Finistère.

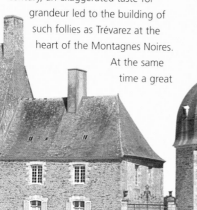

Facing page above: Josselin on the Oust; left: Rochers-Sévigné, rich in literary associations Above: Vitré on the Vilaine

Ancenis

Ancenis was an important castle along the first line of defence of the Duchy of Brittany in the Loire region. Building began in 982. Then, during the 12th century, having married his son Geoffrey to the young Duchess, Henry II of England ruled over Brittany and extended the castle to strengthen his defences. Partly dismantled by Anne of Brittany in 1490, Ancenis was rebuilt at the end of the 16th century. You can still see the fortified walls, the two machi-colated gate towers, the covered drawbridge, and the Grand Logis (residential building) in Renaissance style.
40km northeast of Nantes. Tel: 02 40 83 07 44. Visits by appointment only.

Antrain

Antrain dominates the rivers Couesnon and Loisance from its strategic location on high ground. The village church, built in the 12th century, was fortified in the 15th century to help in the defence of the duchy. The Romanesque front portal is remarkable, with rounded archivolt (ornamental moulding round an arch) and side columns with carved capitals. The domed steeple was added in the 17th century. The decoration of the chancel dates from the 18th century.

Nearby
Château de la Ballue
Erected at the beginning of the 17th century, this castle was one of the main headquarters of the royalist Chouans during the Revolution.
Bazouges la Pérouse, 5km southwest of Antrain. Tel: 02 99 97 47 86.
Open: Apr–Oct (park & exterior only). Admission charge.

Tremblay
In the village is another Romanesque church, remodelled in the 16th century. Note the large cross over the main altar.
4km south of Antrain on the N175.

Antrain is 45km northeast of Rennes on the N175.

Château de Bonne-Fontaine, a 16th-century feudal manor house just south of Antrain

The impressive ruins of la Groulais Castle – still standing despite all Richelieu's efforts to raze it

Bécherel

See p147.

Blain

Blain lies on the north bank of the Nantes-Brest Canal, between Nantes and Redon. The town's commercial tradition goes back to the Roman occupation.

Château de la Groulais

Situated on the south bank of the canal, the castle was built in the 12th century as part of the second line of defence along the border between France and Brittany. Remodelled in the 14th and 15th centuries, the castle belonged to the powerful Rohan family and was partly dismantled in 1628 by Richelieu, whose policy was to eliminate any threat to the king's power.

The ruins include several towers and some part of the walls, the 14th-century keep, and the Logis du Roi, with its high dormer windows and tall red-brick chimneys, typical of Renaissance buildings.
Tel: 02 40 79 07 81. Workshops visits: 20 Jun–25 Sep, 10am–noon & 2.30–6.30pm. Closed: Mon. Admission charge.

Musée des Arts et Traditions Populaires du Pays Blinois

This museum illustrates local history from the Gallo-Roman period with archaeological finds, everyday objects, and a reconstruction of the town's main square surrounded by traditional shops.
2 place J Guihard. Tel: 02 40 79 98 51. Open: 2–6pm. Closed: Mon. Admission charge.

Blain is 38km northwest of Nantes on the D164 to Redon.

Château de la Bourbansais

Built during the 17th and 18th centuries, this impressive residential castle is flanked by two low, round towers and surmounted by the pointed roof of the stair tower. The castle is famous for its French-style gardens and its large open-air zoo.

Like the outside, the interior illustrates the wealth and ambition of the Breton parliament members who built it: exquisite 18th-century furniture, 17th-century Aubusson tapestries, and fine china.
Pleugueneuc, 16km southeast of Dinan on the N137. Tel: 02 99 69 40 07. Open: May–Sep, six guided tours daily. Zoo open: daily, Jun–Sep 10am–3pm. Call for timings during other months.

The remains of the castle at Châteaugiron, often besieged down the centuries

Châteaubriant

Once a major border stronghold, the town developed around its powerful castle, on the banks of the River Chère, and still lives in its shadow.

Château

The castle is in two parts, separated by a formal garden. The medieval fortress, built in the 11th century and surrounded by a fortified wall, includes a massive square keep flanked by the 15th-century Grand Logis and a 13th-century chapel and gatehouse.

The Renaissance buildings were inspired by the beautiful castles of the Loire. They were built by Jean de Laval, Count of Châteaubriant and Governor of Brittany, who is mainly remembered for the gruesome role he played in a tragic story involving his wife, Françoise de Foix. Jealously guarded by a husband she had married at the age of 11, she was lured to the French court and became the mistress of François I. When the king tired of her, she returned to Châteaubriant, who cruelly kept her imprisoned until she died 10 years later. *Rue du château. Tel: 02 40 28 20 90. Open: all year. Guided tours: mid-Jun–mid-Sep 10am–noon & 2–7pm. Admission charge.*

Église St-Jean de Béré

Situated on the other side of the river, this Romanesque church contains several fine 15th- and 17th-century statues and some elaborate altarpieces from the late 17th century.

Châteaubriant is 65km north of Nantes on the D178.

Châteaugiron

The town and its mighty castle were ransacked during the Wars of Religion at the end of the 16th century. However, in the 17th century, the manufacture of canvas brought new prosperity to the town. You can still see some of the half-timbered houses of the merchants, principally along the main street.

Château

The impressive 38-m high round keep, dating from the 13th century, stands apart from the other remaining medieval buildings: the 12th-century chapel, the clock tower and two other 15th-century machicolated towers. The residential building, erected in the 18th century, is now the town hall, which also houses the tourist information office. *Tel: 02 99 37 89 02.*

www.ville-chateaugiron.fr Open: Jul–Aug afternoons; May–Jun & Sep only Sun afternoons. Admission charge.

Châteaugiron is 15km southeast of Rennes on the D463.

Comburg

The romantic figure of Chateaubriand is linked to the town of Combourg, which nestles on the edge of a peaceful lake below an imposing medieval castle. You will get the best overall view from across the lake. With a little imagination, you could recapture the intense, solitary mood that prompted the young Chateaubriand to say later in his famous *Mémoires d'Outre-Tombe*: 'It was in the woods of Combourg that I became what I am today.'

Château

Chateaubriand lived for two years – in almost complete isolation, with his parents and his sister Lucile, his sole companion – in the awe-inspiring fortress. It is no wonder the adolescent Chateaubriand was stirred by it.

Built in the 11th century by the Bishop of Dol, and extended and remodelled in the 14th and 15th centuries, Combourg Castle was bought by Chateaubriand's father; his descendants still live there.

The austere feudal appearance of the castle is marked by four massive towers linked by high crenellated walls. Inside, visitors can see various mementoes of the poet in the Salle des Archives and climb up the 'haunted' Tour du Chat to the bedroom where he listened to the howl of the wind.

Rue des Princes. Tel: 02 99 73 22 95. www.comburg.net Château open: Apr–Sep 2–5.30pm; Oct 2–4.30pm. Closed: Tue. Admission charge. Park open: Jul–Aug daily; rest of the year, Sun–Fri, 9am–noon & 2–6pm. Guided tours: 2pm & 5.30pm.

Combourg is 17km south of Dol-de-Bretagne on the D795.

Dinan
See pp46–7.

Dol-de-Bretagne

This small provincial town was an important religious centre during the Middle Ages, and the starting point of the Tro Breiz (Tour of Brittany), a pilgrimage round Brittany's cathedrals which a Breton felt compelled to make at least once in his life.

Today, pilgrims have been replaced by tourists who come to admire the medieval streets (Grande-Rue des Stuarts and rue Ceinte), lined with half-timbered houses and the wonderful Gothic cathedral.

Cathedraloscope

Halfway between Saint-Malo and Mont-Saint-Michel is the only cultural centre in Europe devoted to the architecture, construction, and symbolism of cathedrals. The viewing platform on the second floor affords wonderful views of the cathedral of Dol-de-Bretagne.
Place de la Cathédrale, 35120 Dol-de-Bretagne. Tel: 02 99 48 35 30; fax: 02 99 48 13 53.
Open: daily, May–Sep 9am–7pm; Oct–Apr 9am–6pm. Free admission.

Cathédrale St-Samson

Erected in the 13th and 14th centuries, the early Gothic edifice shows a strong Norman influence. On the south side a small 13th-century porch offers an interesting contrast with the remarkable 14th-century porch surmounted by a flamboyant balustrade.

The lofty 100-m long nave is impressive, and the chancel is enhanced by beautiful 14th-century stained-glass panels.
Place de la Cathédrale.

Musée Historique de Dol

This museum, featuring local history, includes a fine collection of painted wooden statues going back to the 13th century and small earthenware statues of the 17th and 18th centuries.
4 place de la Trésorerie. Tel: 02 99 48 09 38. Open: May–Oct 9.30am–12.30pm & 1.30–6pm. Admission charge.

Nearby
Menhir de Champ-Dolent

This free-standing stone, set in the 'Field of Grief', is one of the finest megaliths in Brittany. It stands alone in a field, evidence of early man.
1.5km south on the D795.

Mont-Dol

This steep granite mound, 65m high, offers a panoramic view of the whole of Mont-St-Michel Bay.
2km north of Dol on the D155.

Dol-de-Bretagne is 25km southeast of St-Malo on the D4.

Fougères

Once, Fougères was the main border fortress defending the duchy of Brittany and a prosperous market town. Later it became an important centre for the manufacture of canvas. Then, following a slow-down in the canvas industry, Fougères moved successfully into the shoe industry.

Today, wise investments in high-tech industries have enabled the city to flourish once again and restore its architectural heritage.

The slopes of modest Mont-Dol have yielded prehistoric animal remains and human tools

Fougères, an old shoe-making town, found favour with the writers Balzac and Victor Hugo

Medieval Town

The medieval town lies south of the castle. The Église St-Sulpice, built in Flamboyant Gothic style, contains two splendid granite retables and a charming statue of the Virgin Mary feeding her Child. The place du Marchix has been the town's market square since medieval times.

The surrounding streets are lined with 16th-century, half-timbered houses.

Château

Built in the 12th century, the castle stands on a rocky peninsula within a deep bend of the River Nançon. Extended in the 13th, 14th, and 15th centuries, its impressive fortifications, including 13 towers, are remarkable examples of medieval military architecture.

The low but wide south towers facing St-Sulpice church were intended to house heavy guns, and contrast with the 31-m high Tour Melusine built a century earlier.

Past the main gate, a second line of defence barred the entrance to the main courtyard where the residential quarters stood, next to the chapel and the well. The last line of defence protected the keep and the emergency exit.
Place Pierre Symon. Tel: 02 99 99 79 59. Open: mid-Jun–mid-Sep 9am–7pm; mid-Sep–mid-Jun 10am–noon & 2–5pm. Admission charge.

Haute Ville

Situated across the river, the 'high town' dominates the castle and the medieval quarter. At one end of the rue Nationale stands the **Église St-Léonard**, dating from the 16th century, surmounted by a 17th-century tower. Next to it is the 16th-century town hall.

At right angles to the rue Nationale, the rue de la Pinterie leading down to the castle has some 18th-century residences.

The **Musée de la Villéon** is devoted to the Impressionist painter Emmanuel de la Villéon (1858–1954), a native of Fougères.
Rue Nationale. Tel: 02 99 99 19 98. Open: Jun–Sep 10.30am–12.30pm & 2–5pm. Free admission.

Behind the covered market, in the rue Nationale, the Belfry is an interesting octagonal tower, the construction of which dates from the 14th and 15th centuries. However, it is not open to the public.

Fougères is 48km northeast of Rennes on the N12.

Hédé's church is Romanesque and contains a 17th-century alabaster statue of the Virgin

Gâvre, Forêt du
See p141.

Grand-Fougeray
Of its once-powerful castle, there remains one of the most remarkable medieval keeps in Brittany. Built in the 14th century, the tall, round structure has a protruding stair turret linking the four vaulted storeys. It is known as the Tour du Guesclin because it was seized by surprise from the English by Bertrand du Guesclin during the Hundred Years' War.
Tel: 02 99 08 40 19. Open: Jul–Aug 3–7pm. Closed: Mon. Admission charge.

Chapelle Ste-Agathe
In Langon, 12km west on the D56, on the village square next to the Romanesque parish church, stands the small Chapelle Ste-Agathe. Because of its fresco dating from the Gallo-Roman

period, it is known as the Temple of Venus.

Grand-Fougeray is 42km south of Rennes, just off the N137.

La Guerche-de-Bretagne
Since the 12th century, an important weekly market (Tuesdays) has livened the centre of la Guerche. It has 16th- and 17th-century half-timber houses and a partly Romanesque church with a set of beautiful 16th-century choir stalls.
32km southeast of Rennes on the D463.

Hédé
Situated between a lake and the canal linking the rivers Ille and Rance, Hédé village clings to a hill top crowned by a ruined castle. The surrounding area is very attractive, with fine walks. Here you can watch river traffic negotiating a succession of 11 locks with a total difference in level of 27m! The N795 crosses the canal at La Madeleine, which affords the best view of the locks.

Near Hédé are several picturesque villages, including Bécherel (*see p147*), Les Iffs (*see below*), and Tinténiac in a lovely riverside setting, as well as some fine castles: Combourg (*see p37*), la Bourbansais (*see p35*), Caradeuc (near Bécherel), and Montmuran (*see opposite*).
20km northwest of Rennes.

Les Iffs
The village of Les Iffs is famous for the richly coloured stained-glass panels that decorate the Gothic church, in particular those of the chancel depicting the Passion, and, in the south transept, the

martyrdom of St John the Baptist. Dating from the 16th century, they are the works of local craftsmen who were inspired by Dutch and Italian masters.

Château de Montmuran

This well-preserved castle just north of the village is a pleasing blend of austere medieval military architecture and of more refined 17th- and 18th-century domestic architecture. The machicolated gatehouse and drawbridge (in full working order) are quite impressive. The name of du Guesclin is linked to the castle at several points in history: in 1354 he was knighted in the chapel as a reward for his successes against the English; then, as a famous soldier 19 years later, he married the owner, Jeanne de Laval.
Tel: 02 99 45 88 88;
www.chateau-montmuran.com Open: Easter–Oct 2–7pm. Admission charge.

Les Iffs is 8km west of Hédé.

Louvigné-de-Bais

The Gothic church built in the 16th century has superb stained-glass windows, in the finest tradition of Breton craftsmanship, and an altarpiece from the 17th century.

Château de Monbouan

Surrounded by a magnificent park, this charming late 18th-century residence is unpretentious, yet its interior reveals all the grace and elegance of the Louis XV style.

Particularly remarkable within the château are the main stairs, which have been enhanced by a beautiful wrought-iron banister and paintings after Boucher.
5km south by the D777.
Open: mid-Jul–Aug 9am–noon & 2–6pm; guided tours. Admission charge.

Louvigné-de-Bais is 12km southwest of Vitré on the D777.

The ruins of the medieval castle look out over the town of Hédé

The pleasure boat harbour of Redon, where landlubbers can envy the pace and style of life afloat

Abbaye de Melleray

Built on the shores of a lovely lake, Melleray is a Cistercian abbey founded in 1142 and considerably remodelled in the 18th century. The austere Cistercian character of the church has been tempered inside by pink granite pillars and white stone vaulting.

22km south of Châteaubriant on the D178 to La Meilleraye-de-Bretagne, then the D18. Church open: for services only, possible visit to the library; try your luck at the gate.

Château de la Motte-Glain

Built on the edge of a lake by a member of the powerful Rohan family at the end of the 15th century, la Motte-Glain marks the transition between the feudal castle and the residential manor. The machicolations at the top of the elegant gatehouse serve more as a decoration than defence, and the tall dormer windows and conical roofs of the round towers seem designed to make fun of medieval austerity.

La Chapelle-Glain, 20km southeast of Châteaubriant on the D163, then the D878. Tel: 02 40 55 52 01.
Open: guided tours from mid-Jun–mid-Sep 2.30–6.30pm. Closed: Tue. Admission charge.

Paimpont Forest

See p142.

Redon

A relaxed holiday atmosphere permeates Redon, once a busy commercial port at the junction of the River Vilaine and the

Nantes-Brest Canal and now a restful haven for yachts, cabin cruisers and houseboats. The town has gone into floral decoration in a big way along its cobbled streets and bridges, and has several times won first prize in the national Villes Fleuries competition.

Activity reaches its climax on market day (Monday), when crowds of holiday-makers rub shoulders with the locals among the colourful stands.

Part of the old town is pedestrianised, perfect for admiring the splendid 16th-century half-timbered houses along the Grande-Rue and adjacent streets. In the harbour area, the stately three-storey shipowners' houses along quai Duguay-Trouin have lovely wrought-iron balconies and elegant dormer windows. In the rue du Port at the back, you can see the *greniers à sel*, former warehouses used to stock salt from Guérande (*see p127*) on the south coast.

Musée de la Batellerie de l'Ouest
This museum is devoted to the daily life of mariners in the past and includes three barges, two of them afloat.
Quai Jean-Bart. Tel: 02 99 72 30 95. Open: mid-Jun–mid-Sep 10am–noon & 3–6pm. Admission charge.

St-Sauveur
This former abbey church, dating from the 11th century, has a beautiful arcaded Romanesque tower, a blend of strength, simplicity, and artistic inspiration. A fire destroyed part of the nave in 1780, isolating the tall Gothic tower. Note the 17th-century retable in the Gothic chancel. The cloister also dates from the early 17th century.
Place St-Sauveur.

Redon is 66km southwest of Rennes on the D177.

La Roche aux Fées
The peaceful wooded setting helps to surround this impressive prehistoric monument with the kind of poetic mystery that sets the Breton imagination working. In this case it would seem that fairies were responsible for putting together some of the enormous blocks of purple schist, the heaviest weighing 40–45 tons. The fairies went to fetch them in the Forêt du Theil, 5km south, and carried them back in their aprons!
2.5km southeast of Essé and 14km west of la Guerche-de-Bretagne.

La Roche aux Fées has a low corridor ending in a tall room; some rocks weigh up to 45 tons

The rue Beaudrairie, Vitré's most fascinating street, is packed with many curious buildings

St-Aubin-du-Cormier

This small city was the scene of the Duke of Brittany's last stand against the French monarchy in 1488. Beaten and humiliated, he died shortly after the battle, leaving his 12-year-old daughter, Anne, in charge. It was only a question of time before Brittany became a French province.

Today, you can still see the ruins of the formidable castle (not open), whose dismantlement was ordered by Charles VIII after the battle. The mutilated keep stands high above the crumbled walls, a symbol of crushed ambitions.

20km southwest of Fougères on the N12 and 23km northwest of Vitré on the D794.

St-Just

Megaliths of all shapes and sizes are scattered over a wide area of heaths and pine woods around the village of St-Just. Erected around 4500 BC, the megaliths

were in use until the Bronze Age. Long before archaeologists carried out excavations, the Bretons had been inventing poetic legends to satisfy their own curiosity. Thus, Les Demoiselles de Cojoux – a group of three stones, two standing and one on its side – are unfortunate young girls who were turned to stone for having gone dancing on the heath instead of to church.

A network of marked footpaths leads to the Etang du Val, a pretty lake west of St-Just, overlooked by steep rock formations popular with climbing enthusiasts.

8km northeast of Redon on the D177 and D65. Information centre open: Jul & Aug. Guided tours: Wed & Sun. Admission charge.

Vitré

'Were I not the King of France, I would like to be a citizen of Vitré,' declared Henri IV at the end of the 16th century. Although this popular king was fond of making sweeping statements – being a southerner, he was prone to exaggeration – he was obviously impressed.

The well-defended border town became a thriving commercial centre, exporting canvas all over the world, as well as one of the few Protestant towns in Brittany (which partly explains Henri IV's enthusiasm, since he was a Huguenot). The rich merchants' stone and half-timbered houses still line narrow streets such as the rue Beaudrairie and rue d'Embas, close to the castle.

Château

This imposing triangular fortress,

founded in the 11th century but mostly rebuilt during the 13th and 14th centuries, was defended by several towers. The Tour de l'Oratoire houses a 16th-century triptych decorated with enamels from Limoges; the Tour St-Laurent is now a museum that contains a collection of sculptures which belong to various houses in town.

Place du Château. Tel: 02 99 75 04 54. Open: daily, Jul–Sep 10am–6pm; Apr–Jun 10am–noon & 2–5.30pm. Closed: morning Sat–Mon & all day Tue. Admission charge.

Église de Notre-Dame

This 15th/16th-century church contains a remarkable Renaissance stained-glass window illustrating Christ's arrival in Jerusalem. The stone pulpit that decorates the beautiful gabled south wall was apparently built so that the clergy could preach directly to the people and counteract the Protestants' evil influence!

Place Notre-Dame.

Nearby
Château des Rochers-Sévigné

This is where Madame de Sévigné wrote letters to her married daughter. This witty and often sarcastic account of provincial life in the 17th century was later published. The castle contains mementoes of the writer, who used to love strolling in her French garden (designed by Le Nôtre).

6km southeast of Vitré on the D88. Tel: 02 99 96 76 51. Open: Jul–Sep 10am–12.30pm & 2–6.15pm; Apr–Jun 10am–noon & 2–5.30pm. Closed: morning Sat–Mon & all day Tue. Admission charge.

Champeaux

Built by a noble Breton family who had a castle nearby, the church is a rare example of Renaissance art in Brittany, in particular the stained glass and the elaborate funeral monument of Guy d'Espinay and his wife.

9km northwest of Vitré on the D29.

Vitré is 37km east of Rennes on the D857.

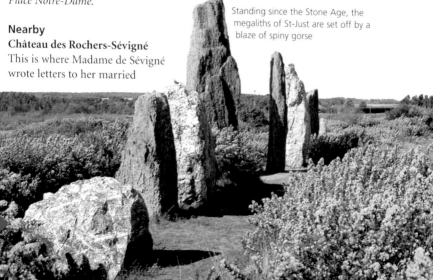

Standing since the Stone Age, the megaliths of St-Just are set off by a blaze of spiny gorse

Walk : Dinan

Still enclosed within its granite walls, Dinan is the best-preserved medieval city in Brittany. A stroll through the old town is like a journey back in time, when Bertrand du Guesclin was trying to boot the English out of France, sometimes single-handedly, and when the young Duchess Anne was trying to keep her duchy.

Allow 2 hours.

Start from the place du Guesclin, where there are parking facilities.

1 Place du Guesclin and Place du Champ

In medieval times, these two adjacent squares formed the city's fairground. In 1357, du Guesclin fought the English knight Thomas of Canterbury in single combat in front of the Duke of Lancaster, who had besieged Dinan. Du Guesclin defeated the knight and thus won the liberation of the city, as well as the admiration of the young Tiphaine, whom he subsequently married. His equestrian statue stands on the place du Guesclin.
Walk along the rue du Château to the castle on your right.

2 Château

Linked to the town walls, the castle consists of a massive oval keep built in the 14th century. It is now a museum housing furniture, tools, costumes and carved wood panels. There is a splendid view from the top.
Return to the rue du Château and continue along the rue du Général de Gaulle. On your left is the Promenade.

3 Promenade de la Duchess Anne

Five centuries on, the 'bonne duchesse' Anne is still remembered with affection in the town where she stayed on several occasions. It is quite conceivable that she strolled along the town walls on a summer evening, just as many visitors do, admiring the view of the River Rance meandering below.
Walk through the Jardin Anglais past the Tour Ste-Catherine and down some steps into the rue du Petit-Fort. Turn right.

4 Rue du Petit-Fort

As the road leads steeply down to the river, notice on your right, at No. 24, a beautiful 15th-century house. Across the Gothic bridge, the old towpath offers a pleasant walk in peaceful surroundings and leads to the village of Léhon, 2km away, where you can see the 12th-century St-Magloire Abbey.
Retrace your steps up the rue du Petit-Fort.

5 Rue du Jerzual

Beyond the Porte du Jerzual (one of the four remaining town gates) is the cobbled rue du Jerzual. Lined with 15th-century corbelled houses with picturesque pointed gables, it presents the colourful scene of weavers, glass-blowers, woodcarvers, and stonemasons at work.

Continue along the rue de la Lainerie, turn left at the place des Cordeliers, and walk past the place des Merciers, at the heart of the most beautiful part of the old town, into the rue Haute-Voie. Turn right opposite the Renaissance Hôtel Beaumanoir.

6 Basilique St- Sauveur

The basilica's mix of architectural styles is particularly striking inside; the right-hand side of the nave is Romanesque, and the left, Flamboyant Gothic. Du Guesclin's heart is said to be kept in St-Sauveur, where it was brought from a church destroyed during the Revolution. *Walk straight to the rue de l'Horloge.*

7 Rue de l'Horloge

On your right is the belfry that houses a 15th-century clock and a large bell, known as Anne, a gift from the young duchess in 1507. On your left is the Hôtel Kératry, a harmonious 16th-century building housing the tourist office. *Turn right into the rue Ste-Claire to return to the place du Guesclin.*

Château Museum
Tel: 02 96 39 45 20. Open: all year daily 10am–6.30pm. Closed: Tue in winter.

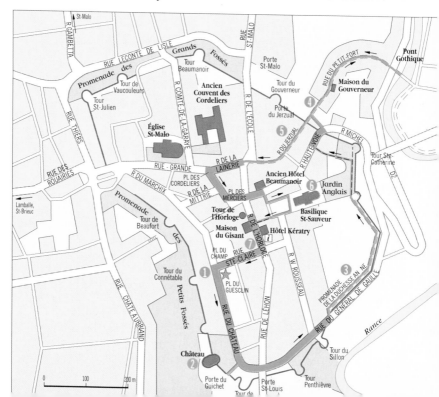

Northern Brittany

Bordering the Channel from Mont-St-Michel Bay to Lannion, and stretching south to Rennes and Mûr-de-Bretagne, northern Brittany roughly fits within the limits of the Côtes d'Armor *département*, except for the short strip of coastline from Cancale to St-Malo, which belongs to Ille-et-Vilaine.

La Baule, Côtes d'Armor

Côtes d'Armor has the most varied coastline in Brittany. Indented by the deep estuaries of the Rance, Trieux, and Jaudy rivers, by wide bays and small creeks, the shores are scattered with huge boulders or lined with fine golden sand,

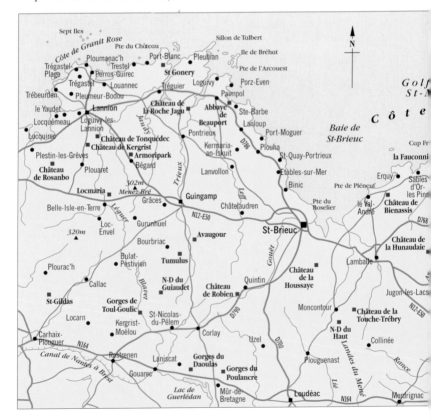

and enhanced by a rainbow of colours suggested by evocative names like Côte d'Emeraude and Côte de Granit Rose. Striking scenery includes the heath on top of Cap Fréhel ablaze with golden gorse, the pink coast of Ile de Bréhat, and the wild Sept Iles teeming with bird life. And twice a day the strongest tidal movements in all of Brittany cause dramatic changes in the landscape.

At the end of the 19th century the north coast of Brittany was already appreciated by holidaymakers from across the Channel, and its popularity has been growing ever since. Resorts range from fashionable Dinard to the family resorts of Perros-Guirec and Trégastel-Plage or the more modest St-Quay-Portrieux – all with beautiful beaches – while modern marinas neighbour traditional harbours.

Maritime Culture

The Côtes d'Armor has a particularly rich cultural heritage: ancient fishing traditions, a turbulent past in the days of privateering, and an exceptional spirit of adventure that opened the way to new territories. All this lives on through annual festive events: *pardons* and folk festivals, and a new determination to use traditional ships in regattas and commemorative events.

Secret Argoat

In contrast, the inland areas of northern Brittany are secluded and peaceful. The countryside is a palette of greens, with small towns of architectural interest such as Moncontour, Quintin, and Jugon-les-Lacs. Here, ancient crafts live on, and a wealth of small chapels waits to be discovered by car, bicycle, on horseback, or on foot.

Le Chemin des Peintres en Côte d'Emeraude

Between Dinard and Cap Fréhel, this unusual open-air museum exhibits some 30 faithful reproductions of famous paintings by Auguste Renoir, Emile Bernard, Pablo Picasso and others, on the spot where they were painted, a great opportunity to view a landscape through the artist's eyes. Information from local tourist offices and Comité Départemental du Tourisme, Office de Tourisme de Rennes, 11 rue Saint Yves 35064 (*tel: 02 99 67 11 11*).

St-Malo

St-Malo has a population of 60,000. It is a thriving commercial and fishing harbour and has a growing ferry traffic with Britain and the Channel Islands. St-Malo is also a popular seaside resort, but it is first and foremost a historic city. Severely damaged in August 1944, it has been faithfully restored.

The Malouins (St-Malo natives) seem to have more than their fair share of the qualities and faults of ordinary Bretons: boldness, determination, and a yearning for freedom. Firmly camped on their rock, they fought to keep in check the ambitions of their powerful French and English neighbours.

The city was named after a Welsh monk, Maclow, who arrived in the 6th century. Shipowners became extremely rich, pursuing St Malo's policy of naval supremacy, while its famous corsairs kept their rivals at bay. Exasperated by the Wars of Religion during the 16th century, the city declared itself a republic until it saw fit to acknowledge the tolerant Henri IV as its lawful king.

Trade with Africa, South America, and India flourished in the 17th and 18th centuries, followed by the golden age of long-distance fishing off Newfoundland and Greenland.

Natives of St-Malo include famous sailors like Jacques Cartier, Duguay-Trouin, and Surcouf, and the writer Chateaubriand (*see box*).

Walled City

Referred to as St-Malo *intra muros*, this is exactly what it is: completely enclosed within formidable walls. Climb the steps by the Porte St-Vincent and walk right round the fortifications. From the top you can see the narrow streets and shipowners' houses in the town; and the harbour, St-Servan, the Rance estuary, Dinard, and Grand Bé Island. Near the oldest (12th century) part of the walls are the statues of Cartier and Surcouf. On the harbour side, the walls date from the 18th century.

FRANÇOIS-RENÉ DE CHATEAUBRIAND (1768–1848)

Chateaubriand was an outstanding literary and political figure of his age, who towered as a writer, philosopher, and man of influence – bold, sometimes unwise, always proud of his Breton heritage. In his *Mémoires d'Outre-Tombe* (*Reflections Beyond the Grave*), he confessed that the sea had been his first love.

A solitary child of emotionally distant parents, he nurtured his imagination for two formative years in the gloomy family castle of Combourg and in the surrounding woods.

He became a leader of the Romantic movement and, by the age of 40, had already achieved international recognition, although his masterpiece, the *Mémoires*, was yet to come.

Chateaubriand died in Paris but was buried, as he had wished, on Grand Bé Island, facing his beloved sea.

St-Malo

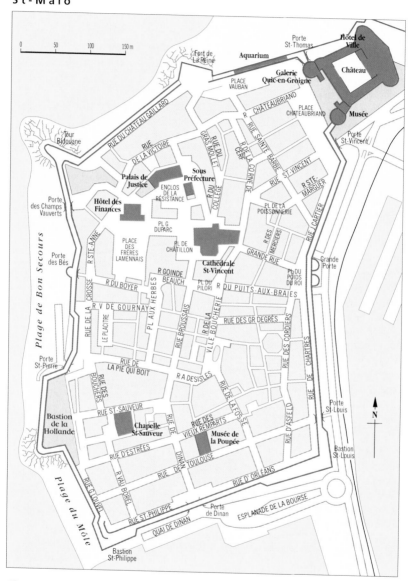

Château

This structure barred access to the city on the land side. The 15th-century Grand

Donjon (Great Keep) houses a museum devoted to the history of St-Malo, while opposite it, the Tour Quic-en-Groigne, a

waxworks museum illustrates St-Malo's glorious past.
Place Chateaubriand, Grand Donjon. Tel: 02 99 40 71 57. Open: Apr–Oct 10am–noon & 2–6pm. Closed: Mon & public holidays in winter. Quic-en-Groigne tel: 02 99 40 80 26. Open: Apr–Oct 9–11.30am & 2–5.30pm, Jul–Aug 9.30am–noon & 2–6pm. Admission charge.

Cathédrale St-Vincent

The cathedral was built between the 12th and 19th centuries, and restored after World War II. The luminous 13th-century chancel inside is decorated with remarkable modern stained glass.
Place Jean de Châtillon.

Fort National

Louis XIV's famous military architect, Vauban, designed Fort Royal in 1689 to reinforce the city's defences. In 1692 it withstood a combined attack by the English and Dutch fleets. The fort was renamed Fort National during the Revolution.
Accessible on foot at low tide. Guided tours only. For information contact the tourist office: Tel: 02 9985 34 33. Admission charge.

Grand Bé Island

According to his wishes, Chateaubriand was buried on this rocky island. A simple granite cross stands atop the anonymous stone under which the writer lies, facing the sea.
Accessible on foot at low tide.

Paramé

The superb sheltered beach stretches from the foot of the castle to the Pointe de Rochebonne, backed by a promenade. There is a fashionable hydrotherapy centre close to the beach.

Rothéneuf

Further northeast along the coast is Rothéneuf, worth a visit for its Manoir Jacques Cartier, the house where the famous explorer settled down in later life. Mainly 15th- and 16th-century, it is furnished in the appropriate style. A video documentary explains how Cartier discovered Canada in 1534.
Limoëlou, rue David McDonald Stewart. Tel: 02 99 40 97 73. Open: Jun–Sep 10–11.30am & 2.30–6pm, rest of the year 9–11am & 2–4pm. Closed: Jun & Sep Mon–Tue; rest of the year, on weekends. Admission charge.

St-Servan-sur-Mer
Corniche d'Aleth

The footpath round the Aleth peninsula affords impressive views of St-Malo, the Rance estuary, Dinard, and part of the Côte d'Emeraude. On the north side is the Fort de la Cité, dating from 1759, which was one of the main defences of the 'Atlantic Wall' during World War II, with blockhouses linked by under-ground galleries.

Tour Solidor

This impressive 14th-century tower, which faces the Rance estuary, was built by Duke Jean IV as a demonstration of strength at the end of the War of Succession, when both the English king and French king had tried to impose conditions on Brittany. It now houses the interesting Musée des Cap-Horniers,

devoted to the epic voyages of the vulnerable ships that sailed round Cape Horn from the 16th century onwards. Navigation techniques, life on board and memorable events are illustrated by means of models, instruments, and mementoes brought back from distant ports of call.
Tel: 02 99 40 71 58. Open: Apr–Oct, daily 10am–noon & 2–6pm; rest of the year till 5pm. Closed: Mon & public holidays. Admission charge.

Mystères de la Mer
This aquarium is a great place to introduce children to the wonders of the sea. There are beautiful sea creatures on show in both underground aquaria and open-air pools. It also boasts the world's only 'nautibus' – a submarine simulator that gives visitors the feeling that they are interacting with (as opposed to observing) life beneath the waves.
Avenue de General Patton. Tel: 02 99 21 19 00. Fax: 02 99 21 12 01. Open: daily, Sep–May 10am–7pm; Jun–Aug 9.30am–10pm. Admission charge.

Nearby
Château du Bos
St-Malo's wealthy shipowners built country houses such as the Château du Bos in the 18th century. The reception rooms still have their original wood panelling, the library contains 6,000 books from the 19th century, and there is a beautiful collection of model ships.

In the extensive park overlooking the River Rance, four statues sculpted out of Italian marble depict the four seasons.
5km south of St-Servan on the N137 and the D5. Tel: 02 99 81 40 11. Guided tours: Jul–Aug 3.30pm & 5pm, Jun & Sep by appointment. Admission charge.

The 14th century Tour Solidor that looks out over the Rance estury

For centuries, life on the rock lying just off the coast of northern Brittany and known as Mont-St-Michel was governed by the clockwork movement of the tides, for the tiny granite island was totally surrounded by the sea at high tide and only accessible at low tide. This dramatic situation, and the mysticism pertaining to its abbey, have contributed to making Mont-St-Michel one of the most visited places in France.

Deposits of sand are threatening to link the island to the mainland but visitors still flock to see the magnificent abbey crowning the top and witness the spectacular tidal movements which, twice a day, alter the landscape in an unforgettable way.

Legend and History

Today's visitors reach Mont-St-Michel by means of a 2-km long causeway built in 1877, but before then thousands of pilgrims crossed the bay on foot at low tide – many perishing in the quicksands or being swept away by the fast-moving tide. However, danger did not deter them, and they kept on coming to fulfil a vow or ask a favour.

The legend began in the 8th century when Aubert, bishop of Avranches, saw a vision of Saint Michael the archangel, who ordered him to build a sanctuary on the island. The sanctuary soon became a place of pilgrimage, with villages all around it.

Several buildings succeeded Bishop Aubert's modest oratory, until history took over from legend with the construction of the Romanesque abbey, replaced and extended later by

superb Gothic buildings collectively known as 'La Merveille' (the Marvel).

The abbey was used as a prison for a while before and after the Revolution, but in 1874 it was entrusted to the care of the Service des Monuments Historiques.

The Abbey

The heavily fortified abbey was never captured, not even during the Hundred Years' War when the English occupied the whole area. From the car park, access is gained by the Porte de l'Avancée: go up the Grande Rue through the walled town, up a series of stairs, and through an imposing gateway.

The abbey church sitting atop the mound is supported by crypts built into the rock. The steeple is surmounted by a statue of Saint Michael 157m above sea level. Inside, the Flamboyant Gothic chancel is magnificent.

On the north side is the splendid Gothic ensemble built on three levels at the beginning of the 13th century, including the remarkable cloisters, where the wealth of poetic expression in the intricate yet harmonious decorations was undoubtedly stimulated by religious fervour.

Strikingly outlined against sky and sea, the abbey of Mont-St-Michel creates a dramatic picture

Belle-Isle-en-Terre

This quiet riverside town is set at the heart of unspoilt countryside where the narrow valleys of the Léguer and the Guic meet. It is surrounded by hills and woods with poetic names like Coat-an-Hay (Day Wood) and Coat-an-Noz (Night Wood), and is well worth discovering without the pressures of time.

Nearby
Locmaria

Overlooking the Léguer Valley, Locmaria Chapel stands at the centre of a small cemetery. A pleasant surprise awaits you inside – a lovely, 16th-century rood screen decorated with painted statues of the Apostles.
1.5km north of Belle-Isle-en-Terre off the D33.

Menez-Bré

From its 302-m summit – pretty high by Breton standards – this isolated 'mountain' affords magnificent views extending north as far as the sea and west to the Monts d'Arrée. The chapel crowning it is dedicated to St-Hervé, one of Brittany's numerous healing saints.
9km northeast of Belle-Isle-en-Terre off the Guingamp road.

Loc-Envel

The unassuming exterior of the Gothic village church does not prepare you for the wealth of decorations within. Every projecting part of the wooden vaulting is adorned with painted sculptures depicting saints, Apostles, and angels, mingling with grotesque figures and fierce-looking animals. A beautiful 16th-century rood screen, a granite altar, and

a stained-glass window in the chancel dating from 1540 complete this profusion of ornamentation.
4km south of Belle-Isle-en-Terre by the D33.

Belle-Isle-en-Terre is 17km west of Guingamp.

Bourbriac

This restful country town owes its name to St-Briac, reputed to heal nervous diseases. At its centre, the church bears witness to the generations of pilgrims who came hoping for a miracle: you can see the stone bench in the 11th-century crypt where the sick used to sit. The crossing (intersection between the nave and transept) is Romanesque, and the tower is transitional in style – the porch being Flamboyant Gothic, and the upper part Renaissance. The church contains a granite sarcophagus said to contain the remains of St-Briac.

Nearby
Notre-Dame d'Avaugour and Notre-Dame de Restudo

Both dating from the 14th and 15th centuries, these are typical of the many delightful chapels to be found at the heart of inland Brittany. Avaugour Chapel contains remarkable carved wooden furniture, and statues of the Twelve Apostles, while the Notre-Dame de Restudo nave and chancel have some interesting 14th-century frescoes.
7km east of Bourbriac, both off the D767 and within 2km of each other.

Bourbriac is 12.5km south of Guingamp on the D8.

Ile de Bréhat

At the centre of an archipelago, Bréhat is surrounded by pink granite reefs glittering in the sun, around which motorboats skilfully wend their way. With a length of only 3.5km and 1.5 at its widest, Bréhat can be discovered on foot or on a bicycle – which is just as well, because cars are not allowed on the island and must be left in the free parking area at the Pointe de l'Arcouest.

The unusually mild climate accounts for the profusion of 'exotic' plants such as mimosas, eucalyptus, and fig trees, and explains why hydrangea flowers brighten up the island's gardens well into October and even November.

The island's only village, known simply as Le Bourg, is in the sunnier southern part, where houses are built of local pink granite. Winding paths lead to various points on the island: St-Michel Chapel on the west coast overlooking Béniguet Island, the vast Baie de la Corderie lined with beautiful villas, and the Rosebo and Paon lighthouses in the wilder northern part of Bréhat.

The locals – just a few hundred, known as Bréhatins – are, like all Bretons, proud of their seafaring traditions and will tell you that, if Christopher Columbus found his way to America, it was thanks to a fisherman from Bréhat who gave him directions!

2km off the Pointe de l'Arcouest, north of Paimpol. Access from Vedettes de Bréhat. Tel: 02 96 55 79 50. For bicycle hire: Tel: 02 96 20 06 26 or 96 20 03 51.

The Gothic-Renaissance tower of Bourbriac's church points commandingly heavenward

Bulat-Pestivien

The splendid church of this modest village points to its importance as a place of pilgrimage in the late Middle Ages. The porch is magnificent, and the Renaissance tower elegant. Inside is an imposing stone table, dating from 1583, on which offerings used to be placed.

Bulat-Pestivien also has three ancient fountains which, like many fountains in Brittany, are associated with both Celtic and Christian rites.
22km southwest of Guingamp on the D787 and D31.

Cancale

To gourmets, Cancale is the name of a fine oyster, *l'huître de Cancale*, which comes from this fishing port on the shores of Baie du Mont-St-Michel – one of the oldest, most important centres of oyster-breeding in Brittany.

Before the 18th century, oysters were plentiful in the bay and much appreciated at court. When stocks began to diminish, a royal decree restricted oyster-fishing to just a few weeks in the springtime.

Oyster-breeding began in the 19th century: young oysters collected from the bay were brought back to grow and fatten in oyster beds. In the 1920s, an epidemic destroyed the supply of young oysters. Today's oysters are imported from the coast of Morbihan, and 3,000 tonnes produced every year. Great efforts are now being made to breed young oysters again in the bay.

The town of Cancale, workaday rather than pretty, overlooks the harbour of La Houle from a plateau. If you see fishermen unload their catch, you may be tempted to buy the oysters for sale on the quayside. Or you can simply watch the fishermen's activity from one of the restaurants.

Quayside colour supplements the bustle of Cancale as it goes about the oyster business

Musée de l'Huître et du Coquillage

This museum of oysters and seashells has a guided tour, with a video documentary on oyster-breeding and an exhibition of more than 1,500 seashells from all over the world.

'L'Aurore'. Route de la Corniche.
Tel: 02 99 89 69 99. Admission charge.

Nearby

Pointe du Grouin

The path known as the Sentier des Douaniers follows the coast to Pointe du Grouin, 7km away: it was earlier used by Customs officers to pursue smugglers. From the top of the 40-m high cliffs, you can admire Côte d'Emeraude and Mont-St-Michel Abbey, or the birds on Ile des Landes.

Cancale is 15km east of St-Malo on the D355.

Châtelaudren

See p147.

Dinard

Known as the 'Pearl of the Emerald Coast', Dinard became a fashionable resort in the mid-19th century, popular with American and English tourists for its fine setting and mild climate. It still retains some of its *belle époque* atmosphere.

Dinard has three lovely beaches. The deep, well-sheltered **plage de l'Ecluse** is backed by luxury hotels, the casino, and the Palais des Congrès. It is linked to the **plage du Prieuré** by the romantic Promenade du Clair de Lune along the Rance estuary. Facing the open sea, the **plage de St-Enogat** nestles below rocks.

Dinard has three golden beaches to choose from

Usine Marémotrice de la Rance

This impressive tidal power station, opened in 1966, harnesses the energy of both the incoming and outgoing tides of the estuary. From there, it is possible to make an interesting round trip by car to Dinan in a day.

3km south on D114. Tel: 02 99 16 37 14.
Open: daily 10am–5.30pm.
Free admission.

Dinard is 25km north of Dinan on the D266 and D766.

Bisquines

Based in Cancale, these traditional fishing boats, rigged with 350sq m of sail, were used to gather young oysters out in Mont-St-Michel Bay. This annual event turned into a real festival of the sea, with some 200 *bisquines* out in the bay at once. A replica launched in 1987, called the *Cancalaise*, is now used for pleasure trips around the bay and to the Channel Islands from mid-March to mid-November. For information, *tel: 02 99 89 77 87.*

Erquy's fishing boats rest by day alongside the cliffs that butt against its popular harbour

Erquy

With its seven sandy beaches, Erquy was one of the first resorts to be developed along the Côte d'Emeraude, and today it is still one of the most popular. The bustling port accounts for much of its appeal. Coastal fishing is the main activity, and the return of the flotilla early in the morning is followed by the noisy auction of the catch in a vast open hall (*vente à la criée*). The speciality is scallops, but, as everywhere along the coast, a great variety of fresh fish is caught and sold immediately to wholesalers and restaurants. The sale takes place every day on weekdays and starts at 7am.

Nearby
Cap d'Erquy

The heath-covered promontory provides shelter for Erquy's many beaches and offers panoramic views of Baie de St-Brieuc as far as Ile de Bréhat.
Cap d'Erquy is 3.5km northwest of Erquy.

Sables-d'Or-les-Pins

'Golden sands and pine trees' – the name itself is an invitation hard to resist. The superb beach faces a group of small islands. One of them, crowned with a chapel dedicated to St Michael the Archangel, is accessible at low tide.
7.5km northeast on the D786 and D4.

Erquy is 33km northeast of St-Brieuc on the D786.

Cap Fréhel
See p73.

Guingamp

Situated between Armor and Argoat, Guingamp has no obvious tourist appeal and most people now take the bypass to reach the coast more quickly. It is a shame, though, not to go through the town and stop, if only long enough to get the feel of the place du Centre and the rue Notre-Dame, the historic heart of the city and today a lively shopping area.

Guingamp is quite modest about its past, yet it had its moments of glory when Brittany was an independent duchy. The Dukes stayed in the castle here, which was dismantled in 1626 by order of Richelieu. Parts of the walls can still be seen on the place du Vally, behind the church.

Notre-Dame-de-Bon-Secours

The Gothic south tower fell down in 1535, taking part of the nave with it. A young architect, Jean Le Moal, rebuilt the south side in Renaissance style, hardly known in Brittany at the time, and decorated the west portal with a

blend of religious and secular motifs. One of the most famous *pardons* takes place here in early July.
Rue Notre-Dame.

Place du Centre

The town's main square is shaded with trees and surrounded by 16th- and 17th-century half-timbered houses. Its triangular shape emphasises its medieval character, and the lovely off-centre Renaissance fountain completes the picture. Known as La Plomée, because it is partly made of lead, it is decorated with rams, dragons, sirens, angels, and dolphins.

Nearby

Armoripark, *see p162.*

Guingamp is 30km northwest of St-Brieuc on the N12.

Château de la Hunaudaye

In ruins but still impressive, the Château de la Hunaudaye is a striking example of what a feudal fortress was like. Even today one can imagine the sense of power its formidable towers must have given its occupants. Belonging to the influential Tournemine family, who backed the losing side in the War of Succession, it was reduced to ruins but rebuilt in the 14th and 15th centuries. Then, during the Revolution, it was

dismantled once again by the Republican army, who feared it might become a Chouan stronghold. During the summer season, life in a medieval castle is re-created by actors in period costumes.
15km east of Lamballe. Tel: 02 96 34 82 10. Open: May–Jun & Sep by reservation; Jul & Aug 11.30am–2.45pm & 4–5.30pm Mon, Tue, Thu & Fri. Closed: Wed, Sat, & Sun. Admission charge.

Jugon-les-Lacs

See p147.

Lamballe

See pp76–7.

Hunaudaye Castle, pillaged for stone until 1930

Lannion

Lannion is within easy reach of the Côte de Granit Rose and of the lovely valley of the River Léguer, famous for its excellent salmon. It's an ideal base for those who wish to sample the different facets of Brittany without driving too many miles: good bathing, superb scenery, green, undulating countryside, and a variety of typical architecture.

Lannion is now a modern telecommunications centre, but several of its tall and narrow old houses – some with corbels and pointed gables, others with mantles of slate – still stand around the church of St-Jean-du-Baly.

Brélévenez Church

The church looks down on the town

Contrasting happily, two old houses in the main square add to Lannion's Breton character

from where it stands on a steep hill. It was built by the Knights Templar in the 12th century and remodelled in the 15th century. You can drive up to the church, or climb the 142 granite steps that lead up to it. Of particular interest are the Romanesque apse and the steeple with its granite spire.
Place E Laurent.

Nearby
Château de Kergrist

A happy blend of styles, this castle has a Gothic north façade and an elegant 18th-century south façade in keeping with the French-style gardens.
9km south off the D11. Tel: 02 96 38 91 44. Open: timings change through the year for gardens and interior; group visits by reservation. Admission charge.

Château de Tonquédec

The ruins clinging to an outcrop overlooking the Léguer are a silent witness of the struggle for power and independence that tore Brittany apart for centuries. This impressive fortress was twice dismantled.
11.5km south on the D31B. Tel: 02 96 47 18 63. Open: Jul & Aug 10am–7pm; other times by appointment. Admission charge.

Léguer Valley

South of Lannion, the Léguer is a fast stream cutting its way through a narrow green valley. The 15th-century **Chapelle de Kerfons** stands like a delicately carved stone jewel in a setting of chestnut trees. The interior contains a wealth of magnificent wood carvings: a flamboyant painted rood screen with statues of the Apostles reminiscent of St-Fiacre Chapel

Brélévenez church, also reachable by car, but without that breathless sense of achievement

(*see p126*) and an extremely ornate retable surmounted by angels.
7km south off the D31B.

Pointe de Séhar
A twisting road follows the south bank of the Léguer estuary through Loguivy, with its quaint parish close dedicated to St-Ivy, to the Pointe de Séhar, which guards the entrance to the estuary and offers extensive views over Lannion Bay.

Lannion is 32km northwest of Guingamp on the D767.

Loudéac
See p77.

Moncontour
See p77.

Mûr-de-Bretagne
A lively market town deep at the heart of inland Brittany, Mûr-de-Bretagne is a convenient starting point for a tour of Lake Guerlédan nearby. But first have a look at the rich interior decoration of the charming Chapelle Ste-Suzanne, which inspired Corot.

Lac de Guerlédan, Brittany's largest lake

Lac de Guerlédan

This sinuous lake, the largest in Brittany, fits so well into its wooded surroundings that it is hard to believe it was artificially created when a dam was built across the Blavet in the 1920s.

Past the village of St-Aignan and its charming 12th-century church, a minor road cuts through the Forêt de Quénécan. Wood from the forest was used in the Rohan family's ironworks of Les Forges des Salles; their ruined castle is close to the village.

Further on, near a lock on the River Blavet, stand the ruins of the Cistercian **Abbaye de Bon Repos**. North of the river, the River Daoulas goes through a narrow gorge on its way to join the Blavet, and a pleasant shaded road runs alongside. Boat trips and water sports are available from Beau Rivage.

Mûr-de-Bretagne is 17km north of Pontivy on the D767.

Paimpol

Yachts and cabin cruisers are moored here today, but graceful schooners first brought fame to this town. Paimpol is known now mainly for coastal fishing and oyster-breeding, but in days gone by it was closely linked with cod-fishing. Up to 80 schooners would leave port together, bound for North Atlantic waters scattered with treacherous icebergs, and hundreds of fishermen, known as Les Islandais, died off the coasts of Newfoundland and Iceland.

The quiet of place du Martray, and its austere, stately granite houses with carved embrasures, is a marked contrast to the confusion of colourful boats in the harbour just a few steps away.

Paimpol-Kerity, 3km south on the D786. Tel: 02 96 20 81 59. Open: Jul & Aug 10am–noon & 2–7pm. Admission charge.

Loguivy
Set amid pink granite rocks, this pretty lobster-fishing village has inspired writers and painters.
5km north on the D15.

Pointe de l'Arcouest
On the way down to the vast parking area are remarkable views of the sea scattered with islets and reefs. The island of Bréhat (*see p57*), glittering in the distance, is a 10-minute ferry ride away.
9km north on the D789. Ferry shuttle service to Bréhat every hour.

Paimpol is 45km north of St-Brieuc by the D786.

Perros-Guirec
See pp74–5.

Plestin-les-Grèves
Close to one of the best beaches on the north coast is the pleasant holiday resort of Plestin-les-Grevès, which offers exciting possibilities of excursions. The church contains the grave of St Efflam, a 5th-century Irish missionary.

The magnificent beach of Lieue de Grève, just 3km northeast, is at least 4km long. The sea withdraws over a distance of 2km twice a day, to the immense delight of children and cockle-gatherers.

At the western end of the beach is the St-Efflam Chapel, which marks the spot where the holy man landed.

Musée de la Mer
This maritime museum traces the history of fishing off the coast of Iceland. In addition, an authentic fishing boat rescued from the scrapyard is now permanently moored in the harbour: the *Mad Atao* serves as a floating museum and historic monument.
Museum: rue de la Benne. Tel: 02 96 22 02 19. Open: Easter & mid-Jun–mid-Sep 10am–noon & 3–7pm. Admission charge.
Mad Atao open: Jun–Aug 2–8pm. Free admission.

Nearby
Abbaye de Beauport
Built in the 13th century close to the sea, the abbey was in use until the Revolution. Hydrangeas grow among the imposing ruins.

Roche-Jagu Castle, atop steep wooded slopes, has exhibits and displays in summer

Nearby
Corniche de l'Armorique
Beyond St-Efflam begins the indented Corniche de l'Armorique, well worth exploring as far as Locquirec. From the Pointe de Plestin there is a splendid view of the Lieue de Grève. Beyond, the road skirts a stream and leads to the charming fishing port and family resort of Locquirec.
West along the D42 and D64.

Plestin-les-Grèves is 18km southwest of Lannion on the D786.

Pontrieux
Pontrieux developed as a bridge town at the head of the Trieux estuary and as a safe port of call for merchant ships. But eventually the town found itself too far from the sea and, having outlived its usefulness, its growth came to an end. The result is a delightful small town with a wealth of domestic architecture from the 16th to the 19th centuries.

Château de la Roche-Jagu
This fully restored 15th-century castle, overlooking a bend in the River Trieux 60m below, defended the river – no doubt very effectively, as you can see if you follow the watchman's round on the river side.

The interior gives a good idea of life in a medieval castle, with metre-thick walls and numerous massive fireplaces.

6km north off the D787.
Tel: 02 96 95 62 35. Open: guided tours
(ring beforehand): Jul & Aug 10am–7pm;
other months 10am–6pm.
Admission charge.

Pontrieux is 17km north of Guingamp on
the D787.

Quintin
See p77.

Château de Rosanbo
Little remains of the original 'rock on
the (river) Bo' built in the 14th and 15th
centuries. The present castle is an
elegant 17th- and 18th-century manor
house looking out on to French-style
terraced gardens designed by Le Nôtre.
Inside there are fine pieces of furniture,
Aubusson and Flemish tapestries, and a
library that once belonged to Louis
XIV's finance minister.
Lanvellec, 20km southwest of Lannion on
the D786 and the D22. Tel: 02 96
35 18 77.
Open: Apr–Jun,
weekends 2–5pm;
Jul & Aug, weekends
11am–6pm; Sep, Sun
only 2–5pm.
Admission charge.

St-Brieuc
St-Brieuc is
both a historic
town and the
modern
administrative
and commercial centre of the
département of Côtes d'Armor, with
regular markets and trade fairs.

The city was founded in the 5th
century by Brieuc, a Welsh monk and
one of the seven founders of Brittany. A
15th-century fountain in the rue
Ruffelet marks the place where Brieuc
built his monastery. In medieval times
pilgrims flocked to the town, which was
on the route of the Tro Breiz (holy tour
of Brittany).

The town was attacked and destroyed
during the War of Succession, the Wars
of Religion, and the Chouan rebellion,
and unfortunately little of the old town
has survived. Most of the remaining old
corbelled houses are to be found in the
picturesque streets north of the
cathedral: the rue Fardel leading to the
place du Lin, the rue Quinquaine, rue
du Parc, and rue du Gouët (James II of
England lodged here in 1689).

Cathédrale
Dating from the 13th and 14th centuries,
the massive fortified edifice bears
witness to the city's troubled
past. From the front it looks
like a medieval castle, its
twin towers reinforced
by buttresses and
defended by

Encrusted with
lichen, this wild
boar in pink
granite stands
outside
Rosanbo's 14th-
century façade

machicolations. The lofty nave was rebuilt in the 18th century. Notice the beautiful stained-glass window in the south transept and the Renaissance organ loft.
Place du Général de Gaulle.

Nearby

North of St-Brieuc and the River Gouët, cliffs and beaches alternate along the coast. From the **Pointe du Roselier**, rising 70m above sea level, the view extends across the wide bay of St-Brieuc and south to the **Anse d'Yffiniac**, where the tide sometimes recedes over 7km, revealing clusters of black mussels clinging to thick wooden posts.

Further north, there are two lovely and safe beaches, **Martin-Plage** and **Les Rosaires**, the latter 2km long.

Binic, once an important port connected with cod-fishing in the North Atlantic, is today a charming seaside resort with three good beaches and a large marina.
St-Brieuc is 99km northwest of Rennes on the N12.

St-Nicolas-du-Pélem

St-Nicolas is situated in the upper valley of the Blavet and is an area of considerable scenic beauty. Woods, chaotic groupings of boulders, streams, and lakes make it ideal touring country for those who like the peace and quiet of minor roads and small villages.

In the chancel of the 15th- and 16th-century church are two lovely stained-glass windows depicting the Passion. Alongside the church is a charming 17th-century fountain, named after the patron saint of the village.

Nearby
Gorges de Toul-Goulic

The River Blavet disappears with a thundering noise under a tumble of huge boulders in wooded surroundings.
9.5km northwest of St-Nicolas on the D50 and the D87. The site is a 10-minute walk from the car park.

Kergrist-Moëlou

As is often the case in Brittany, the imposing Gothic church is out of proportion with the modest size of the village. The south side is richly decorated; 500-year-old yews and an impressive calvary complete the picture. Dating from 1578, the calvary was partly destroyed in 1793; a closer inspection reveals that some of the characters were repositioned incorrectly!
17km west of St-Nicolas on the D87.

St-Nicolas is 44km southwest of St-Brieuc on the D790.

St-Quay-Portrieux

You would think that a modern family seaside resort like St-Quay – with its superb bathing, brand new harbour, fun and entertainment for all ages – would surely not be linked with legend. But you wouldn't be in Brittany if there were no legend attached to the place!

The town was named after an Irish monk called Ké, who arrived a long time ago in a stone trough. Beaten by local women and left badly wounded on the shore, he prayed for help, and was healed, finding refuge under a gigantic bramble bush.

When the chapel built on the spot was destroyed in 1875, a huge bramble was found under the altar. All Bretons will assure you that the story was passed on to them by their great-grandmother, who heard it from an eyewitness!

You can walk along the Sentier des Douaniers, which follows the coast from the harbour to the plage du Châtelet, for good views of the Bay of St-Brieuc.

Nearby
Côte du Goëlo
Northwest of St-Quay-Portrieux, the coast is a succession of cliffs and creeks, like the picturesque Port Moguer. Allied aircrews, shot down over France during World War II, escaped back to Britain from the plage Bonaparte.

Kermaria-an-Iskuit
In the chapel, a realistic 15th-century Dance of Death, depicting the living holding hands with the dead, is said to have prompted Saint-Saëns to compose his *Danse Macabre*. *11.5km northwest of St-Quay.*

St-Quay-Portrieux is 18km north of St-Brieuc.

Tréguier
The city has a number of old houses dating

from the 15th to 18th century, including philosopher Ernest Renan's birthplace, but the city's main claim to fame is the magnificent cathedral which dominates the centre of the old town.

Founded by St-Tugdual, one of Brittany's seven founders, the town developed within the Jaudy estuary and soon became a powerful bishopric and an important centre of learning. But, curiously enough, its strongest

The Chapel of St-Quay-Portrieux

St-Tugdual
Cathedral, one
of the finest in
Brittany

associations are
with another saint:
Yves, a lawyer, a
priest and an
advocate of the
poor, who lived in
the 13th century
and is still
honoured
every year
in May in
one of the most important *pardons* in
Brittany.

Cathédrale St-Tugdual
This splendid pink granite building
radiates a strong spirituality unaltered
by the passing of time. It is, essentially,
an imposing Gothic edifice dating from
the 14th and 15th centuries; all that
remains of the
Romanesque

Wide stretches of sand shelve gently into the sea, making le Val-André popular with families

cathedral is Hastings Tower over the north transept, while the spire on the south tower is 18th-century.

To the north of the nave is St-Yves's tomb, dating from the 19th century, a copy of the medieval tomb destroyed during the Revolution. In the south transept is a statue of the saint between the rich and the poor, and 46 beautiful Renaissance stalls in the chancel.

Under the Romanesque arches of Hastings Tower, a door leads to the beautifully preserved Flamboyant cloister. In the vestry, you can see the relic of St-Yves, which traditionally leads the procession during the famous *pardon*.

Nearby
Port-Blanc
A pleasant seaside resort with a wide beach, sand dunes, and an interesting 16th-century Gothic chapel.
9km northwest on the D70 and D74.

Tréguier is 29km north of Guingamp on the D8.

Le Val-André
This popular resort has one of the finest beaches on the north coast. You can see birds nesting on the island sanctuary of le Verdelet, off the Pointe de Pléneuf and accessible at low tide.

Nearby
Château de Bienassis
This fortified castle dating from the 15th and 17th centuries, complete with moat and crenellated wall, is still inhabited.
7km northeast off the D786.
Tel: 02 96 72 22 03. Open: Jun–mid-Sep 10.30am–12.30pm & 2–6.30pm, other times by appointment. Closed: Sun morning.

Le Val-André is 26km northeast of St-Brieuc on the D786.

Tour: Côte d'Emeraude

This tour includes one of the most famous landmarks in Brittany, as well as seaside resorts, beaches, promontories, and, as a contrast, the ancient walled town of Dinan.
Allow a full day.

Start from Dinard (see p59) and follow the D786 west.

1 St-Lunaire

This fashionable resort lies at the base of

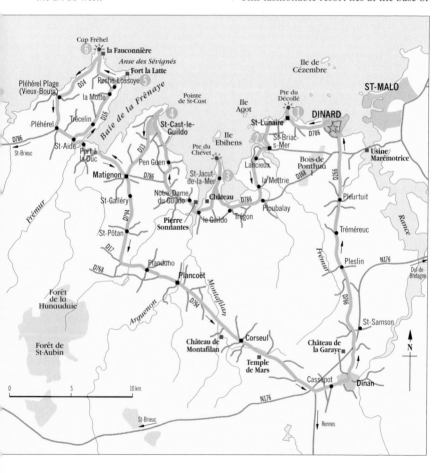

a tiny peninsula with a lovely beach on either side. The tip of the peninsula is known as the Pointe du Décollé; linked to the rest by a natural bridge spanning a deep crevice, it offers striking views of the whole of the Côte d'Emeraude. *Continue along the D786.*

2 St-Briac-sur-Mer

St-Briac is a different kind of resort, with a lively yet relaxed atmosphere, a traditional fishing harbour, a convenient marina, and several lovely beaches. *Coming out of St-Briac, follow the cliff road to the new bridge across the Frémur, which has good views of the resort; 7km further on, turn right on the D26.*

3 St-Jacut-de-la-Mer

This fishing village and seaside resort is camped on a narrow peninsula jutting out into the bay, with a fine beach and a cliff near the tip. Ile Ebihens lies just beyond. *Double back to rejoin the D786 (which you will leave again a few kilometres further on), past the Arguenon estuary; look for the* bouchots à moules *(wooden posts used for mussel-breeding). Turn right on the D19.*

4 St-Cast-le-Guildo

St-Cast is one of the main resorts along the coast, ideally situated between two rocky promontories sheltering a beautifully curved beach. From the Pointe de St-Cast to the north there are panoramic views of the Emerald Coast. *Leave St-Cast along the D13 towards Matignon and turn right; the road skirts the Baie de la Frênaye. Turn right on the D16.*

5 Fort la Latte

About 60m above the pounding waves, this medieval castle faces the open sea, dominating the cliff top. A path leading to the entrance passes a slim Neolithic menhir and continues on to two drawbridges spanning deep crevices. The massive round keep stands on a rocky mound inside the second courtyard. From the top the view extends east as far as St-Malo. *Drive northwest to Cap Fréhel.*

6 Cap Fréhel

This is one of the most famous sights in Brittany, with breathtaking scenery unfolding from the edge of the 70m-high cliff. Colonies of sea birds nest on the rock face and whirl round with deafening shrieks. Go to the very tip of the promontory, beyond the lighthouse; then follow a path down to a terrace to observe the birds at close range. *Follow the scenic D34 across the heath and turn left after 5km to rejoin the D786. Turn left again, then right at Matignon and follow the D794 to Dinan (see pp46–7). Drive north along the D766 to return to Dinard.*

Fort la Latte *Tel: 02 96 41 40 31.* Open: Apr–Sep 10am–12.30pm & 2.30–6.30pm. Admission charge.

Gargantua

This mythical giant lived on the heath near Cap Fréhel. One day, on his way to St-Malo, he stopped to remove a 'pebble' from his shoe and threw it away – it broke up into the reefs below Cap Fréhel. He then paused for a drink, planting his stick in the ground at Fort la Latte. It has remained there to this day as a menhir known as Gargantua's Finger.

Tour: The Corniche Bretonne

Strangely-shaped pink rock formations with even stranger names are the attraction along this stretch of coastline. The tour is only 30km long but shouldn't be rushed: there's a great deal of pleasure awaiting you on a stroll round the municipal park in Ploumanac'h, a walk from Trégastel across to Ile Renote, or round the moors of Ile Grande.
Allow half a day.

Start from Perros-Guirec.

1 Perros-Guirec

This is an ideal family resort, with sheltered shallow beaches particularly safe for children, a sophisticated hydrotherapy centre, and plenty of entertainment, including a casino. It is also a good central base from which to explore the Côte de Granit Rose, or to

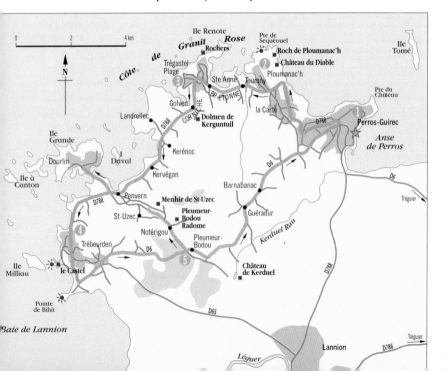

take a boat trip round the Sept Iles bird sanctuary. The church is quite interesting inside: the first part of the nave is Romanesque with round pillars that are plain on the left, decorated with engaged columns on the right, and surmounted by capitals carved with Celtic motifs.
Leave Perros-Guirec by the D788 towards Ploumanac'h.

2 Ploumanac'h

A path runs along the beach where St-Guirec landed in the 6th century (there is a small oratory nearby), then disappears through huge pink boulders and enters the municipal park. Follow the path round until you reach the Château du Diable, which looks like a forbidding ruined castle, then turn right to return to the car park.
Continue on the D788.

3 Trégastel-Plage

The setting of this small resort is memorable: fine sand beaches are backed by huge, wind-eroded boulders (some with individual names), while the sea is scattered with small islands. Let your imagination run free when you look at the 'Witch' or 'Death's Head' or the 'Pile of Pancakes', but don't worry about the precariously perched 'Die' – it's been like that for literally ages! A narrow sandbank links the Ile Renote to the mainland, with more rocks piled chaotically.
Turn south towards Trébeurden. About 1.5km further on, turn left, then right to reach the Dolmen de Kerguntuil, which has an interesting covered passage. Return to the main road and continue south. The coast is particularly attractive until Penvern; from there you could make
a detour to Ile Grande and walk round the island, which is covered with wild moors.

4 Trébeurden

This popular seaside resort has several south-facing beaches. Walk to le Castel for good views of the coast and of the Ile Milliau (accessible on foot at low tide, otherwise by boat), with a wealth of flora and fauna. Further south, the Pointe de Bihit offers a panoramic view of the Baie de Lannion and a vast beach below.
Drive east on the D6 to Pleumeur-Bodou and turn left.

5 Pleumeur-Bodou Radôme

Since 1962 this huge white ball, 64m in diameter, has been an important centre of satellite communications when the first ever transatlantic TV broadcast was received here via Telstar. Next door, a museum illustrates the history of telecommunications. There is also a vast planetarium showing 10 different programmes at fixed times, varying with the seasons.
Continue a little further on the road to Penvern to admire a huge standing stone, the Menhir de St-Uzec, surmounted by a crucifix. Return to Pleumeur-Bodou and turn left on the D6, which takes you back to Perros-Guirec.

Pleumeur-Bodou Radôme
Tel: 02 96 46 63 81. Open: May, Jun, & Sep 10am–6pm, Jul & Aug 10am–7pm, other months, afternoons only. Closed: Sat. Admission charge. For further information, contact Musée des Télécommunications, *www.leradome.com*
Planetarium de Bretagne
Tel: 02 96 15 80 30 for details.

Tour: Ancient Towns of Central Brittany

This tour takes you through the heart of Argoat – inland Brittany – with its forests, undulating hills, and solitary heaths. Above all, you are introduced to its small peaceful towns.

Allow a full day.

Leave St-Brieuc on the N12 going east.

1 Lamballe

Now a little hillside town of whitewashed houses, this former capital of the duchy of Penthièvre played a considerable political role until the Revolution – and sometimes had to pay dearly for it. It

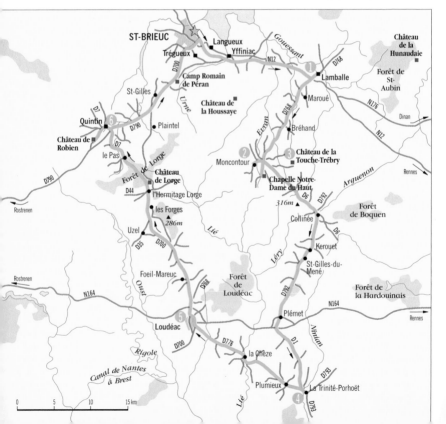

was saved from economic decline by the Haras National (national stud farm), founded in 1825; it keeps 400 horses.
Follow the D768 south.

2 Moncontour

A mark of Moncontour's prosperous past as a centre of the hemp and linen industry are the superb houses of merchants and craftsmen round the place de Penthièvre and in the rues du Temple and des Dames; notice the beautiful carvings decorating some embrasures. The 16th-century church of St-Mathurin is beautifully lit by six fine stained-glass windows, inspired by Flemish artists.
Take the D6 towards Collinée and turn left after 3km along the D25.

3 Château de la Touche-Trébry

The castle stands in a secluded spot between a wood and a lake. Surrounded by a moat and a fortified wall, it looks like a feudal castle although it was built in the late 16th century.
Rejoin the main road and drive to Collinée, then turn right on the D792, cross the N164 and continue on the D1.

4 La Trinité-Porhoët

A fine Romanesque-Gothic church graces this sleepy little town nestling in the valley of the Ninian. The beautiful church portal is framed by slender columns with delicately carved capitals. Over the main altar, an interesting retable illustrates the Tree of Jesse.
Follow the road to Loudéac, stopping at la Chèze to visit the captivating regional museum of Breton crafts – Musée de Bretagne.

5 Loudéac

Loudéac is an important market town, but it's also well-known for its horse-racing events in spring. The Église St-Nicolas, rebuilt in the 18th century, contains an unusual main altar set beneath a *baldachin* (canopy).
Drive north on the D700, then bear left on the D7 to Quintin.

6 Quintin

In the 17th and 18th centuries, Quintin experienced a sudden boom through its linen trade. Today, the town presents an architectural harmony of stately houses rising in terraces above the river. Built on the edge of a lake, the castle is in two parts: the first part (17th century) remains unfinished; the second (18th century) houses a museum of local history.

The Notre-Dame Basilica, rebuilt in the late 19th century on the site of the previous church, contains a precious relic brought back from Jerusalem by Crusaders in 1252: a fragment of a belt said to have belonged to the Virgin Mary.
The D790 and D700 take you back to St-Brieuc.

Château de la Touche-Trébry *Tel: 02 96 42 78 55. Open: Jul–mid-Sep 2–6pm.*
Closed: Sun. Admission charge.
Haras National Place du Champ de Foire. *Tel: 02 96 50 06 98. Open: all year 2.30–4.30pm. Free admission.*
Musée de Bretagne *Tel: 02 99 28 55 84.* Open: all year 10am–noon, 2–6pm.
Closed: Tue & public holidays. Admission charge.
Quintin Château and Musée *Tel: 02 96 74 94 79. Open: mid-Mar–May 2–5pm.*
Closed: Jun–Oct, Tue 1.30–6.30pm. Admission charge.

Fishing and Oyster-Breeding

One of the main attractions of Brittany is its many fishing ports. The drone of diesel engines signals returning craft and heralds a sudden burst of activity. Fishermen in yellow oilskins bustle about the decks, selling the day's catch right on the quay. Locals make judicious remarks, auctions proceed noisily in overcrowded halls. In the mid-afternoon lull, brightly coloured boats bob gently with the breeze.

Best of all, as you stroll along in the quiet of the evening, is the irresistible smell of grilled fish coming from small quayside restaurants. But, of course, such an appealing picture is founded on a way of life.

and Iceland, for tuna in the Indian Ocean, and for lobster off the coasts of Portugal, Morocco, and even Brazil. These ever-longer voyages coincided with the development of preservation techniques. Today, most large ports specialise in what is called 'industrial' fishing. Concarneau sends floating factories to fish for tuna off the coast of Africa, while Douarnenez, Audierne, and Camaret-sur-Mer specialise in lobster-fishing. Along the north coast, St-Malo is the only port to uphold the

Seawater in their Veins
Every Breton is a fisherman at heart, ready to defy the hardships and dangers of looking for cod off the coasts of Newfoundland

tradition of cod-fishing off the coast of Canada, since Paimpol and neighbouring ports have turned to scallop-fishing in St-Brieuc Bay. But smaller ports continue the ancient daily pattern of netting a variety of local fish, supplying the needs of discerning palates of native and visitor alike.

Farming the Seabed

Brittany is a major source of shellfish, particularly oysters. There are two kinds: the native flat oysters and the less refined Portuguese or Japanese oysters, which were imported when an epidemic killed the majority of native oysters.

Oyster-breeding began in Brittany more than 150 years ago. The technique involves covering tiles with lime and laying them in sheltered bays or river estuaries to attract young oysters. Later

these are transferred to oyster-beds (*parcs à huîtres*) until they mature three or four years later. They are then sold or placed in specific places, such as the Bélon estuary, to improve their taste. The particular balance of fresh water and sea water in the River Bélon results in the highly acclaimed flavour.

Top: a fine specimen in Concarneau's fish market, below: flat-bottomed boat used for oysters and mussels

Finistère

The westernmost of Brittany's four *départements* has a strong sense of its own identity, evolved over the centuries from the close relationship between the people and their natural environment. Bretons have fought an ongoing duel with the elements, to achieve survival while making a living out of the sea.

Heavy work: off-loading a good catch of crab

The names given to some of the most dangerous spots – such as the Baie des Trépassés (Bay of the Dead) or Nouveau Cimetière (New Cemetery) – reveal the people's fear of their ancient adversary, but imply as well an acceptance of the risks involved in their way of life, which they readily defend. For the people of Finistère (the name derives from *finis terrae* – land's end) have had a long-standing love affair with the sea. They mourn their dead and curse the cruel sea, but generation after generation has answered its call.

The Coast of Legends, in northwest Finistère, is broken up by *abers* indenting the land

Finistère confronts the sea on three sides, and its irregular coastline points to the struggle in which wind and waves endlessly reshape the land. To the north there are sand beaches, dunes, and *abers* (shallow estuaries invaded by the sea at high tide but looking like mud flats at low tide). The west coast bears the brunt of the Atlantic's assault. Its cliffs have crumbled into the sea, forming a scatter of dark shiny reefs, and a succession of peninsulas and promontories face barren, austere islands that are often hidden in mist. Treacherous navigation has resulted in this part of Brittany having the highest concentration of lighthouses in France – 23 in all.

Finistère's south coast is far more welcoming. Sheltered harbours and sunny coves of fine sand hint at the long sandy beaches found in Morbihan and Loire-Atlantique further south and east.

Rugged Land, Strong Convictions
Inland Finistère has more variety than any other part of Brittany. Besides its rivers, green valleys, and forests, it has in its centre the only Breton mountains – mere hills by ordinary standards, but so rugged and austere that one quickly forgets their modest height. It is here,

surrounded by uncompromising Nature, that the Breton temperament was inspired to a corresponding religious fervour unmatched elsewhere in Brittany, and the result can be seen in its unique parish closes (*see pp98–101*).

Finistère has guarded its Breton culture even more jealously than other parts of Brittany. Fishing is still the main occupation – and the main political issue – along the coastal fringe, which has two of the largest fishing ports in France

(Douarnenez and Concarneau) as well as a string of smaller but very active ones, like Guilvinec.

More people speak the Breton language here than anywhere else, and lifestyles are most strongly rooted in the past. Cornouaille, the south-western part of Finistère, has been known as the bastion of traditional Brittany since the 19th century, when painters such as Paul Gauguin found inspiration in the landscapes and its people.

Finistère

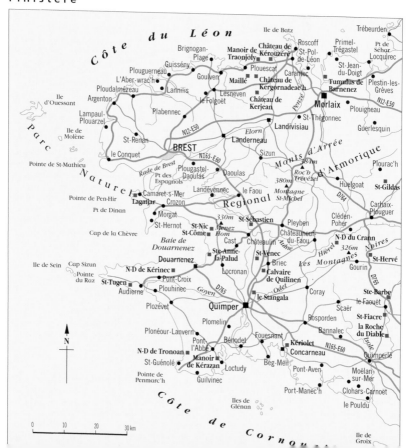

Quimper

Back in the 5th or 6th century, upriver from the Gallo-Roman settlement of Aquilonia, Bretons chose the confluence of the Odet and Steir rivers as the site for their new city; this location also determined its name (*kemper* means confluence).

Tiles announce Quimper's pottery

Gradlon, legendary 6th-century ruler of the drowned city of Ys and first king of Cornouaille, is supposed to have made Quimper his new capital, with his friend Corentin as its first bishop. The town walls and the cathedral were erected in the 13th century, but the city really began to develop during the Revolution, when it became the administrative centre of Finistère.

Today, Quimper carries out its dual role of administrative centre and ancient capital with a great deal of inventiveness. Its exceptional architectural heritage blends harmoniously with new creations like the Halles (Market Hall) at the heart of the old quarter and the Maison du Département (County Hall) on the River Odet. Far from being a museum piece, Quimper bustles with the excitement of a modern city, its streets suddenly swelling at lunch time with business people. Yet, more than any other town, it seems imbued with Breton culture, symbolised by the elegant granite spires of the cathedral soaring above old timber-framed houses.

From Mont-Frugy, a small hill on the south bank of the Odet, there are lovely views of this 'City of Art' nestled in its steep-sided valley.

Cathédrale St-Corentin

This fine, imposing building dates from the 13th and 15th centuries. In 1239 it was decided to replace the existing Romanesque cathedral and work began on the chancel, but war and lack of funds delayed its completion until 1410. The nave and the towers are 15th-century, but the spires were added in 1856 and modelled on that of Notre-Dame-de-Roscudon in Pont-Croix (*see pp86–7*). If you stand back from the cathedral, you will see between the towers an equestrian statue of King Gradlon – a typically Breton link between religion and legend. Walk round to the north side to admire the flying buttresses and the porch.

Inside you will immediately notice that the nave is not in alignment with the chancel; this is probably due to technical difficulties during construction. The 15th-century stained glass of the upper windows is remarkable. The pulpit, dating from 1679, is decorated with scenes from St-Corentin's life, and the organ, from 1643, is by Robert Dallam, an English organ-maker of some repute.

Musée Départemental Breton

Created in 1846, the museum is now in the old bishop's palace, between the

cathedral and the river. A veritable treasure, it is devoted to Brittany's past, featuring archaeological collections with a section on prehistory and the Gallo-Roman period, and various items illustrating Breton religious art from the 12th to 17th centuries, including some painted wooden statues. There are also beautiful regional costumes, furniture, and, last but not least, a unique collection of Quimper ceramics (*see p154*) from the 18th century to the present day.
1 rue du Roi Gradlon. Tel: 02 98 95 21 60. Open: daily, Jun–Sep 9am–6pm; Oct–May 9am–noon & 2–5pm. Closed: Mon & Sun morning. Admission charge.

Quimper is situated 220km west of Rennes and 250km northwest of Nantes and connected by fast dual carriageway; 100km south of Roscoff, linked by ferry to Plymouth and Cork. Direct rail link to Paris by TGV (fast train). Daily flights from Paris to Quimper Pluguffan Airport; regular flights from Cork from April to September.
Office de Tourisme: Place de la Résistance. *Tel: 02 98 53 04 05*. Open: Jul & Aug 9am–7pm, rest of the year 9.30am–12.30pm & 1.30–6.30pm.

The cathedral's spires soar above the town

Musée des Beaux-Arts

Situated on the north side of the cathedral, the recently renovated Fine Arts Museum is one of the finest of its kind outside Paris. Two rooms on the ground floor are devoted to Breton paintings of the 19th century, including *Une Noce en Bretagne* (Breton Wedding) by Leleux and *Champ de Foire à Quimper* (Fairground in Quimper) by Perrin. Another room is devoted to Max Jacob, a native of Quimper, and his friends Picasso, Cocteau, and others.

The extensive collection of Breton paintings continues on the first floor with the Pont-Aven School, including *Etudes de Bretonnes* (Breton Women) by Emile Bernard, *La Vieille du Pouldu* (Old Woman from Le Pouldu) by Sérusier, and *Paysage de Pont-Aven* (Landscape from Pont-Aven) by Maufra. The Nabis and Symbolists are also represented; notice, in particular, *Pardon en Pays Bigouden* (Pardon in Bigouden Country) by Lionel Floch. The 20th century is represented by Delaunay, Marquet, Derain, and many others; particularly striking is the life-size reconstruction of the dining room of the Hôtel de l'Epée in Quimper, decorated with Breton scenes by Jean-Julien Lemordant between 1905 and 1909.

Other rooms on the first floor contain Italian paintings from the 14th to the 18th century, Dutch and Flemish paintings of the 17th and 18th centuries, including works by Rubens and Jordaens, as well as a vast collection of French paintings from the 17th to the 19th centuries, including famous works by Boucher, Fragonard, Corot, and Boudin.

40 place St-Corentin. Tel: 02 98 95 45 20. Open: Jul & Aug 10am–7pm, rest of the year 10am–noon & 2–6pm. Closed: Tue & Sun morning. Admission charge.

Musée de la Faïence

The Ceramics Museum traces 300 years of pottery-making in Quimper (*see p154*).

A vast collection of more than 2,000 pieces, shown in rotation, are decorated with religious and historical themes, scenes of daily life, or abstract motifs. The items exhibited illustrate the evolution of the craft and the blending of famous styles from other French regions such as Rouen, Nevers and Moustiers. The manufacturing process is

St-Corentin Cathedral has a number of stunning stained-glass windows from the 15th century

Café society, leaving the Gauloise-scented fug at the bar to enjoy the fresh air and sunshine

clearly explained with samples of the tools and raw materials used.

14 rue JB Bousquet. Tel: 02 98 90 12 72. Open: Apr–Oct 10am–6pm. Closed: Sun. Admission charge.

Nearby you can also see the ceramic works of HB Henriot; each piece is hand-painted and signed by the artist.

Rue Haute. Tel: 02 98 90 09 36. Open: Mon–Fri 9–11.30am & 1.30–4.30pm (Fri till 3pm).

Notre-Dame-de-Locmaria

Standing on the south bank of the River Odet, this Romanesque church was part of a Benedictine monastery. The interior is quite bare apart from a rood beam bearing Christ wrapped in a robe.

Nearby
Chapelle de Kerdévot

This beautifully located 15th-century chapel contains a Flemish retable which tells the story of the Virgin Mary.

8km east of Quimper on the DI5.

Quilinen and St-Venec Calvaries

These two calvaries were undoubtedly carved by the same craftsmen, for they both have an unusual triangular base. This device allows the statues to be placed on different levels, thus naturally drawing the eye upwards to the top of the cross.

8km north off the D770 and 5km further on the same road.

Site du Stangala

From the parking area, a path leads through the woods right to a natural terrace which overlooks — from a height of 80m — a bend in the River Odet.

6km north on a minor road branching off the D15 to Coray on the left.

Les Abers

The low-lying coastal area of northwest Finistère is known as the Pays des Abers (*aber* country) because its rocky coastline is punctuated with estuaries called *abers*. Nothing like the deep Rance or Trieux estuaries of the north coast, they are in fact the shallow outlets of small streams. A common sight is the many small boats left stranded in the mud at low tide.

The sea here is scattered with reefs, and navigating can be tricky in spite of the numerous lighthouses. However, several picturesque harbours such as L'Aber Vrac'h, Portsall, Porspoder, and Lanildut still pursue age-old activities, essentially local fishing and the gathering of *goémon* (seaweed) used as a fertiliser. Particularly plentiful in this area, you can see it drying on the sand dunes of Ste-Marguerite peninsula, between Aber Vrac'h and Aber Benoît, which has lovely views of both.

Further south, a pretty road follows the coast closely between Trémazan and Argenton; here you can see the notorious Roches de Portsall, on which the oil tanker *Amoco Cadiz* ran aground in 1978, causing the worst pollution ever seen on the coast of Brittany.

Montagnes d' Arrée

See Parc Naturel Régional d'Armorique, p143.

Audierne

Situated at the entrance of the Goyen estuary, Audierne is today a medium-size fishing port specialising in lobster and crawfish; the catch is stocked in seawater pools that can be visited. Some of the large trawlers that used to fish off the coasts of Portugal, Morocco, and even Brazil now rest in a ships' graveyard on the banks of the River Goyen.

Nearby
Pont-Croix

This ancient market town is famous for its 13th-century church, the Notre-

Shellfish are the mainstay of Audierne, which also boasts a large, sandy beach

Dame-de-Roscudon, whose splendid architecture has had a long-lasting influence: four centuries later, its 67-m spire was the model for those of St-Corentin Cathedral in Quimper. Most remarkable is the south porch, with its three delicately carved gables.
5.5km northeast on the D765.

Le Marquisat
Decorated like an olden-days Breton home, this is a fascinating glimpse into the past.
Le Marquisat, Pont Croix. Tel: 02 98 70 51 86. Open: Jul–Sep 10.30am–12.30pm & 3.30–6.30pm.

Ile de Sein
This unassuming patch of flat land, at the mercy of the ocean's wrath, is steeped in legend – no doubt because a ring of treacherous reefs and violent currents make for difficult access. In Celtic times it was the final resting place of the mystical Druids, but for generations now it has been home to fishermen and their families.

On the western side of the island, the sea is so rough that the Ar Men lighthouse, which stands on an isolated reef, took 30 years to build at the end of the 19th century. The island entered French history books in 1940, when the entire male population crossed the Channel to join Général de Gaulle's Free French Army in Britain.
23km west of Audierne. Regular boat service from Audierne-Ste-Evette; sailing time 1 hour. No cars allowed.

Audierne is 36km west of Quimper on the D784.

A curving, south-facing beach adds to the appeal of Bénodet, at the mouth of the Odet

Bénodet
This elegant seaside resort at the entrance of the Odet estuary has three beaches, a casino, and a vast marina packed with yachts. From the centre, the avenue de Kercréven leads to a wooded area overlooking the harbour, the estuary, and the pretty Pont de Cornouaille. From the bridge are striking views of Bénodet harbour and Ste-Marine opposite.

Nearby
The tiny hamlet of **Le Letty** lies on the shores of the peaceful laguna called Mer Blanche, ideal for safe sailing (instruction available).
4km on the D44 east and minor road south.

Bénodet is 15km south of Quimper; boat trips up-river to Quimper and to Iles de Glénan.

Brest

Brest is undoubtedly the most prestigious of French ports, associated with the country's maritime history from the colourful days of the Royale (French navy in the past) to the more sombre events of World War II, when the city was totally destroyed.

The new town that emerged from the ruins has wide avenues and vast open spaces and is once again France's major naval port on the Atlantic. Its shipyards build the largest warships in France, such as the aircraft carrier *Charles de Gaulle*, the latest to be launched. In addition, Brest has taken on the new roles of university town and oceanographic research centre.

Château

Situated at the mouth of the Penfeld estuary, the castle was miraculously spared by the bombs of the last war and now stands as almost the only reminder of Brest's past. Built in the 12th century but later remodelled, it houses an extensive maritime museum.

From the castle, the cours Dajot, built on the old town walls, affords views of the whole harbour.
Tel: 02 98 22 12 39. Open: 10am–noon & 2–6pm. Closed: Tue. Admission charge.

Musée des Beaux-Arts

The most interesting exhibit of this Fine Arts Museum is its collection of works by painters of the Pont-Aven School, including Emile Bernard and Paul Sérusier.
29 rue Traverse. Tel: 02 98 00 87 96. Open: 10–11.45am & 2–6pm. Admission charge.

Océanopolis, Brest's outstanding sea centre

Océanopolis

This new oceanographic centre, resembling a giant architectural crab, takes you on a journey into the ocean's depths with the help of huge aquariums, the largest in Europe.
Port de Plaisance du Moulin Blanc. Tel: 02 98 34 40 40. Open: daily May–Sep 9am–6pm. Admission charge.

Pont de Recouvrance

An impressive piece of engineering, the bridge has a main span of 87m and rises 26m to allow ships in and out of the Penfeld estuary.

Tour Tanguy

Facing the castle is the city's only major relic of medieval times. Now the tower functions as the Musée Municipal du Vieux Brest, preserving the memory of pre- and post-Revolution Brest.
Opposite the castle on the river Penfeld. Tel: 02 98 00 86 31. Open: Jun–Sep 10am–noon & 2–7pm. Free admission.

Brest is 70km northwest of Quimper on the fast N165 dual carriageway.

Brignogan-Plage

This popular seaside resort in north Finistère lies at the centre of the Côte des Légendes, known locally as Pagan Country, a surprising term considering the number of chapels and granite crosses strewn about the countryside.

The people of ancient Léon had the reputation of being less friendly than other Bretons; one legend even tells how at night they would tie lanterns to the horns of their cows to lure passing ships on to the reefs. Today, the coastal fringe forms part of the Ceinture Dorée (Golden Belt), and produces great quantities of onions, cauliflowers, artichokes, and other vegetables.

At Brignogan, sandy beaches alternate with large rock formations. On the way to the Pointe de Pontusval nearby, you can see an 8-m high menhir (standing stone), a base for a cross. Interesting cycle trips in the area include the ancient village of Goulven (7km south) and Guissény resort (9km southwest).

33km northeast of Brest on the D788 and the D770.

Carantec

Carantec has all the ingredients which are necessary to make a family holiday a memorable success: sea, sand, and scenery. Occupying a prominent position inside the Bay of Morlaix, its curve of sheltered beaches is interrupted to the northeast by picturesque cliffs facing the 16th-century Château du Taureau, and several small islands (now the protected nesting grounds of thousands of birds).

Gourmets will appreciate the fresh supply of oysters from the oyster beds south of Pointe de Pen-al-Lann near the Plage du Clouet.

To the northwest lies Ile Callot, accessible on foot at low tide, with its sandy creeks as well as outcrops of granite.

15km northwest of Morlaix on the D73 and the D33.

The view over a Carantec beach from the rocky platform known as La Chaise du Curé (Priest's Chair)

Châteaulin: angling takes place downstream of the town, whose coat of arms features a salmon

Carhaix-Plouguer

In Gallo-Roman Brittany, Carhaix-Plouguer was a thriving trading town and the capital of what is now Finistère. The well-preserved bridge on the River Hyère, just north of the city, dates from that period. Today, it is an important dairy centre.

Like all self-respecting Breton towns and villages, Carhaix has its hero, and its legend. The hero is a modest Breton (an unusual combination), known as La Tour d'Auvergne, who repeatedly distinguished himself in Napoléon's army, but refused promotions and medals. He was made First Grenadier of the Republic by Bonaparte himself

shortly before dying in action in 1800. His memory is honoured every year in June.

The legend is somewhat gruesome. Many centuries ago, there was a local bluebeard who, fearful about being killed by a son, killed each wife as soon as she was with child. The fifth wife saved her child with the help of St-Gildas, but eventually the bluebeard discovered his child, and had him beheaded. Then along came St-Trémeur, who picked up the head and carried it to the bluebeard's castle. He threw a handful of sand at the castle, whereupon it crumbled to dust. A statue of St-Trémeur with the boy's head stands over the fine Gothic portal of the Église St-Trémeur. Inside, there is a beautiful Renaissance altarpiece.

Nearby

There are two charming parish closes at **Cléden-Poher** and **St-Hernin**, with particularly fine calvaries.
9km southwest of Carhaix-Plouguer.

Carhaix-Plouguer is 46km southwest of Guingamp on the D787.

Châteaulin

This sleepy riverside town, on the edge of the Parc Naturel Régional d'Armorique, is a famous salmon-fishing centre. Traditional granite houses, neatly lining the embankments, are reflected in the still waters of the canalised River Aulne.

A parish close stands among the ruins of the castle, overlooking the river and the town. An arched gateway leads to the Église Notre-Dame (once the chapel of Châteaulin castle), recently restored and graced by a slender Renaissance tower. The calvary dates from the 15th century and the ossuary, adjacent to the church, from the 16th century (access from the rue Graveran).

Nearby
Ménez-Hom
From its isolated position, the 330-m high mountain peak offers exceptional views of Baie de Douarnenez, the Crozon Peninsula, Cap Sizun, and, closer, the Aulne estuary, and the Pont de Térénez.
15km west of Châteaulin on the D887, then right on the D83.

Chapelle St-Côme
Beautifully proportioned, this rural chapel boasts elegant carvings of floral and animal motifs along the cornice at the base of the vaulting.
19km west of Châteaulin on the D887, then the D108 and the D63.

Châteaulin is 30km north of Quimper on the N165 dual carriageway.

Concarneau
One of France's most important fishing ports, Concarneau specialises in tuna caught off the coast of Africa and processed in three local canneries. Its delightful harbour has been guarded since the 14th century by the famous Ville Close (Walled City). Built on a small island barring the entrance to the harbour, the Ville Close is completely surrounded by defensive walls and towers. From the top of the walls, a fine view extends over the fishing port with its vast *criée* (auction hall) and the marina on the other side.

Boat trips are available to the Glénan island of St-Nicolas (1 hour 10 minutes) and to Beg-Meil across the Baie de la Forêt (30 minutes). The Pointe du Cabellou, facing the entrance to the harbour, is a good place for a scenic cycling tour.

Musée de la Pêche
This comprehensive museum – part inside, part outside the old walls – covers all activities associated with fishing, including shipbuilding, canning, and sea rescue.
Rue Vauban. Tel: 02 98 97 10 20.
Open: mid-Jun–mid-Sep 9.30am–7pm, rest of the year closed for lunch.
Admission charge.

Concarneau is 21km southeast of Quimper on the D783.

The isolated, barren peak of Ménez-Hom takes on the colours of sunset every evening

In the parish close of Daoulas, three sides of the elegant 12th-century cloister still stand

Crozon Peninsula
See pp110–11.

Daoulas
Now a cultural centre, the village is famous for its abbey, which was founded in the 6th century and rebuilt 600 years later. The abbey prospered until the Revolution. The buildings we see today are from different periods. A 16th-century porch marks the entrance to the parish close. The former abbey church has kept its Romanesque west front and imposing nave. The cloister, unique in Brittany, has 32 Romanesque arches, varied ornamentation, and, in the centre, a stone basin decorated with curious grotesques. In the grounds are a medicinal plant garden, a 16th-century fountain, and a small oratory.
Tel: 02 98 25 84 39. Open: summer, daily 9am–7pm; rest of the year, weekdays 10am–noon & 1.30–5.30pm. Admission charge.

Daoulas is 20km southeast of Brest on the N165.

Douarnenez
Sardine-fishing brought prosperity to this historic fishing port in the mid-19th century, when canneries employed a great number of women. Next came lobster-fishing along the coast of Africa. Now Douarnenez divides its efforts between local and long-distance fishing to keep its high rank among the fishing ports of France. Visit the harbour at night, when the day's catch is being unloaded.

There is superb scenery round the bay here, which enclosed the legendary town of Ys, submerged by the sea (*see box*). This is a watersports centre, with sailing schools, surfing, and beaches a few kilometres away. Part of the old harbour has recently been turned into a museum, unique in Europe. From the marina at the entrance of Port-Rhu, a path follows the coast past Tristan Island (where the famous lovers Tristan and Isolde are said to have taken refuge), skirts the Plage des Sables Blancs and leads to the Pointe de Leydé, which offers panoramic views of Douarnenez Bay.

Port-Musée
Housed in a former cannery, the museum is devoted to traditional boats of all kinds and sizes from all over Europe. In the fascinating open-air section along the quayside of Port-Rhu, the floating part of the museum re-

creates the colourful harbour animation of the past. At present, only three of the boats can be visited.
Place de l'Enfer. Tel: 02 98 92 65 20.
Open: daily 10am–7pm.
Admission charge.

Douarnenez is 23km northwest of Quimper on the D765.

Le Faou

Gabled houses with slate-covered façades, dating from the 16th century, line one side of the high street of this charming old village. The church has a richly carved south porch. Le Faou is a good starting point for excursions to the Crozon Peninsula and the Montagnes d'Arrée.

Nearby
Landévennec Abbey
The ruins of the Benedictine abbey, founded in the 5th century by the Welsh monk Gwennolé, have a lovely rural setting

The Drowned City of Ys
Some 1,400 years ago, King Gradlon lived in the beautiful city of Ys, on the shores of Douarnenez Bay. His daughter led such a dissolute life that God sent a handsome stranger to punish her. The stranger tricked her into giving him the keys that opened the dikes protecting the city from the sea, and the waters flooded into the city. Woken by St-Guénolé, the king jumped on his horse with his daughter, but St-Guénolé ordered him to let go of her, and she met a watery end. In good weather, fishermen still claim to hear the bells of Ys ringing beneath the sea.

at the entrance of the Aulne estuary. The church is said to contain the grave of King Gradlon (*see box*). A museum illustrates the abbey's history.
21km west of le Faou on the D791 and D60. Tel: 02 98 27 35 90. Open: daily, May–Oct 10am–7pm; Nov–Apr 2–6pm. Closed: Tue. Admission charge.

Le Faou is 32km southeast of Brest off the N165.

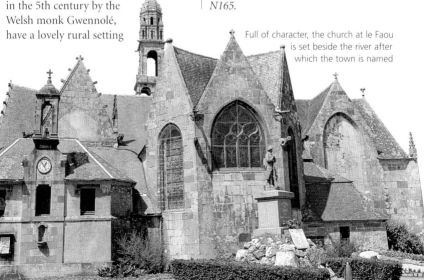

Full of character, the church at le Faou is set beside the river after which the town is named

Le Folgoët

Famous for its splendid basilica and its *pardon* in September – one of the most important in Brittany – this modest village and pilgrimage centre owes its name to yet another legend. Folgoët means 'Madman's Wood', and the madman in question was a poor simpleton who lived near a spring on the edge of the forest and could say only two words: Ave Maria. When he died, a white lily grew on his grave bearing those very words in gold letters. A church dedicated to Our Lady was built over the spring. The building was completed in 1423.

Notre-Dame Basilica

The most striking feature of this massive Gothic basilica is undoubtedly the granite rood screen, admirably proportioned and delicately carved. At the east end of the building, against the chancel wall, a fountain is fed by the spring running beneath the altar.

Le Folgoët is 23km northeast of Brest on the D788.

Fouesnant

This very pleasant little town, set among fruit orchards on the Baie de la Forêt, produces the best cider in Brittany, according to the locals. In its sheltered position on the west side of the bay, Fouesnant is dotted with wooded sand dunes. During the Fête des Pommiers (Apple Tree Festival), in July, you can see women wearing their exquisite lace headdresses, each one unique to its district with its own particular shape.

Nearby
La Forêt-Fouesnant

This idyllic village, at the end of a deep bay, is a popular sailing and walking

The 16th-century Pont de Rohan, in Landerneau, is one of the last inhabited bridges in Europe

area. Its charming parish close has an interesting 16th-century calvary, and the typically Breton church a slender granite steeple.
3.5km northeast of Fouesnant.

Fouesnant is 15km southeast of Quimper on the D45 and the D34.

Guerlesquin
See p147.

Huelgoat
See p142.

Château de Kerjean
This splendid example of 16th-century architecture caused Louis XIII to proclaim it 'one of the handsomest houses in the kingdom'. Surrounded by double ramparts and a moat, the Renaissance-style castle influenced other constructions in the area, including the famous parish closes. Partly destroyed by fire in 1710, it was bought by the State in 1911 and restored, except for the right wing.

It contains a remarkable collection of ancient Breton furniture. In the vast grounds, a park covering 20 hectares, are a charming fountain and a superb dovecote.
10km north of Landivisiau. Tel: 02 98 69 93 69. Open: summer only 10am–7pm. Closed: at 6pm on Fri. Admission charge.

Landerneau
Landerneau is one of those estuary towns that prospered from the 16th century through a thriving export trade with Spain and Portugal. The pictures-que bridge spanning the River Elorn was built by the Rohan family, who once owned the town.

The town is now the commercial centre of a rich agricultural area. On the place St-Thomas on the left bank is the Église St-Thomas-de-Cantorbéry, with its curious three-tiered steeple. A small Renaissance ossuary stands nearby.
20km northeast of Brest on the D712.

Locronan
This gem of a village presents a remarkable ensemble of Renaissance domestic architecture, the heritage of its prosperous days as a centre of sailcloth manufacture. Time seems not to have touched medieval Locronan, and it can look strangely like a ghost town. Dedicated craftsmen keep alive the skills of woodcarving, glass blowing, and weaving in wool, linen, and silk.

The imposing church dominating the main square is dedicated to St-Ronan, an Irish hermit who lived in a nearby forest and used to climb barefoot up a nearby hill, the Montagne de Locronan. During the July *pardon* (called a *troménie* here), the procession of pilgrims follows in the saint's footsteps.

Nearby
Ste-Anne-la-Palud
The 19th-century chapel of Ste-Anne stands among sand dunes on the shores of Douarnenez Bay. Every year at the end of August, the area is invaded by a colourful crowd attending one of the most famous *pardons* in Brittany.
8km northwest of Locronan on the D63.

Locronan is 10km east of Douarnenez on the D7.

Shopping or just strolling is a pleasure to be savoured in the streets of old Morlaix

Montagnes Noires

Together with the Montagnes d'Arrée in the north, the Black Mountains form the east-west backbone of Brittany. Written across a map, 'Montagnes Noires' may seem a pompous designation since the highest summit is only 326m, but the expansive vistas, the outcrops of sombre rock and a dark mantle of forest justify the term — with a little imagination, of course!

The small towns of Gourin and Châteauneuf-du-Faou are good starting points for a sightseeing trip. Gourin was once a thriving town, the centre of slate extraction, but part of its population emigrated to America during the 19th century. A few kilometres northwest on the D301, you can climb the highest peak, the Roc de Toullaëron, from where the view extends far and wide.

The idyllic setting of Châteauneuf-du-Faou appealed to Paul Sérusier, one of Gauguin's friends who decorated one of the chapels in the church. For amateur anglers the location overlooking the River Aulne is a paradise. South of the river lies the **Domaine de Trévarez**, combining outdoor and cultural entertainment (*see p142–3*).

Morlaix

Morlaix occupies the bottom of a deep, almost canyon-like valley, spanned by a huge viaduct casting its shadow on the town. The long estuary, known as the Rivière de Morlaix, provided a means for the export of linen cloth famed all over Europe, which ensured Morlaix's prosperity for nearly 500 years. The harbour expanded downriver, where rich shipowners built stately homes along the quayside. In the 18th century, Morlaix was almost as famous for privateering in merchant shipping as St-Malo. Today, the harbour shelters a more peaceful flotilla of yachts.

The medieval town lies at the foot of the viaduct, which carries the main Paris-Brest railway line. Along the pedestrianised Grand Rue and the narrow streets known as *venelles*, there are still many timber-framed corbelled houses, built between the 15th and the 17th century. The most famous is the Maison de la Reine Anne in the rue du Mur, decorated with statues of saints and grotesques.

Not far away is the **Église St-Mathieu**, rebuilt in 1824 and worth a visit for its medieval statue of the Virgin and Child, which opens up like a triptych.

Musée des Jacobins
Housed in a former church, the museum contains archaeological finds, a fine collection of Breton furniture and some interesting religious statues.
Place des Jacobins. Tel: 02 98 88 68 88. Open: 10am–12.30pm & 2–5pm (6pm in summer). Closed: Tue. Admission charge.

Morlaix is 60km northeast of Brest on the N12 dual carriageway.

Ile d'Ouessant
Separated from the mainland by one of the strongest tidal currents in the world and often surrounded by a veil of mist, Ouessant is a holiday centre known for its rugged terrain: the once cultivated land is now virtually treeless and sheep graze freely there.

But the island seems to have found a promising new source of income – the farming of seaweed. As part of the Parc Naturel Régional d'Armorique, Ouessant also promotes a new kind of tourism, emphasising the discovery of nature and the rediscovery of old traditions.

Ecomusée
Two traditional houses, containing furniture, costumes, and domestic tools, illustrate daily life on Ouessant in the past.
Niou Huella. Tel: 02 98 48 86 37. Open: May–Sep 10.30am–6.30pm, rest of the year afternoons only. Closed: Mon. Admission charge.

Musée des Phares et Balises
Appropriately located in a lighthouse, the museum is devoted to the history of lighthouses and their keepers since ancient times.
Phare du Créac'h. Tel: 02 98 48 80 70. Open: as for Ecomusée. Admission charge.

Access by boat from le Conquet (1 hour), by air from Brest (15 minutes).

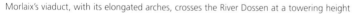

Morlaix's viaduct, with its elongated arches, crosses the River Dossen at a towering height

The Christianising of Druidic standing stones, surmounting them with crucifixes or carving Christian symbols on them, was an early sign of the religious evolution of the Bretons, a deeply spiritual people. This evolution gained momentum over the centuries to culminate in an explosion of artistic creation, whose greatest expression was the parish close. These unique architectural entities flourished in Brittany – and more specifically in and around the Elorn Valley – with the flowering of the Renaissance, between the 15th and the 17th centuries. They recall a time when everyday life centred around the parish.

both outside and inside, with elaborate christening fonts and pulpits, luminous rood beams and beautiful altarpieces. Ossuaries, originally leaning against the church, gradually assumed the new role of funeral chapels and became separate buildings. Near the church, and often in front of it, stands the calvary, a direct descendant of those simple crosses erected by the wayside, in fields or facing the sea. The elaborate calvaries, known all over the world as a distinctive feature of Breton religious art, are often remarkably complex; designed to instruct a largely illiterate population, they are like a three-dimensional Bible with as many as 200 characters displayed round a solid granite base.

A Message in Stone

Situated at the heart of the village, the close is entered through a monumental gate usually leading straight into the cemetery and symbolising access to eternal life. The church stands at the centre, small but profusely ornamented

An Invitation to Meditate

Like the great medieval cathedrals, these grey stone parish closes combine the spiritual and the aesthetic in a way that defies indifference. For the strong beliefs of a people are there in front of our eyes, carved in local granite: their conviction that eternal life can be

touched through a
beautiful work of art, their
blend of realism with an
inclination towards the
supernatural, their love of
powerful symbols. But
there is more: parish closes
express a belief in social
order and in the need to
perpetuate that order
through teaching.
They also suggest the
desire of a
community
to assert its
religious identity
for all
posterity.

Facing page top:
detail of calvary of
Rochefort-en-Terre;
below: porch
ornamentation,
Guimiliau
Above: Guéhenno's
calvary; left: calvary
of St-Thégonnec

Parish Closes

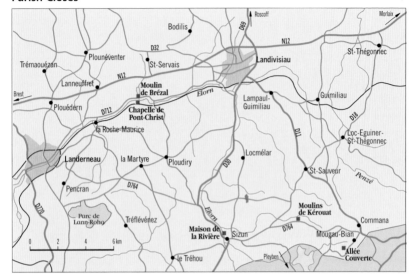

Parish Closes

The concentration of parish closes in a relatively small area lends itself to a convenient day trip, starting from Landerneau or from Landivisiau.

Guimiliau

The striking calvary offers a complex yet harmonious arrangement of 200 characters over an arched base, depicting scenes from the life of Jesus and from His Passion. The church interior is also remarkable and includes a christening font beneath a baldachin, a finely carved pulpit, and a 17th-century organ.
7.5km southeast of Landivisiau on the D11.

Lampaul-Guimiliau

Here the artists concentrated on the church. A feast of colours welcomes you inside: the rood beam decorated with a frieze in a lively Naïve style, the

magnificent retable in high relief, the elegant baptistery, and a beautiful *pietá* carved from a single piece of wood.
4km southeast of Landivisiau on the D11.

La Martyre

This small village has the oldest parish close in the area, with the calvary set on top of the gate. Note the lovely south porch of the church and the extensive interior decoration.
6km southeast of Landerneau.

La Roche-Maurice

The church contains a rare Renaissance rood screen and a 16th-century stained-glass window throwing light on the main altar. Above the holy water basin outside the ossuary, Death threatens a group of people with an arrow, saying '*Je vous tue tous*' ('I kill you all)'.
4.5km northeast of Landerneau on the D712.

St-Thégonnec

For two centuries, there was intense rivalry between St-Thégonnec and Guimiliau nearby, each town trying to surpass the other in splendour.

The result is a remarkable church and an ossuary chapel. Note particularly the domed Renaissance tower of the church and, inside, the richly-carved pulpit that dates from 1683.

9km east of Landivisiau on the N12 dual carriageway.

Sizun

With its triple arch and Corinthian columns, the monumental gate is reminiscent of Roman ceremonial arches. Note also the 16th-century ossuary chapel, with its small museum.

12km southeast of Landerneau on the D764.

There is another famous parish close further south in Pleyben, near Châteaulin (*see pp90–91*). The calvary has a truly monumental base, although the whole is not so harmonious as in Guimiliau.

Plougastel-Daoulas

This small town is the commercial centre of the Plougastel peninsula, famous for its strawberries and early vegetables.

The calvary, built between 1602 and 1604 after an epidemic of plague had devastated the area, ranks among the finest in Brittany. It suffered bomb damage in 1944, but was restored a year later thanks to the generosity of an American officer.

10km east of Brest on the N165.

Pont-Aven

This small river port prospered as a mill town and acquired international fame when a group of artists – later known as the School of Pont-Aven – gathered there round Paul Gauguin (*see pp102–3*). Delightful riverside walks around the town take you along the Promenade Xavier Grall up to the Bois d'Amour, and in the other direction towards the harbour; they include marked paths that identify the locations of famous paintings. On the outskirts of town stands the Chapelle de Trémalo. Its crucified Christ served as the model for Gauguin's famous *Le Christ Jaune* (The Yellow Christ).

Musée

Apart from its permanent collection of works by the Pont-Aven group (none by Gauguin himself), the museum illustrates life in the town in Gauguin's time with the help of old photographs.

Place de l'Hôtel de Ville. Tel: 02 98 06 14 43. Open: Apr–Dec 10am–12.30pm & 2–7pm. Admission charge.

Pont-Aven is 14km east of Concarneau on the D783.

The River Aven once powered many mills, but is now at the service of Pont-Aven's boat users

Gauguin and the School of Pont-Aven

When Gauguin arrived in Pont-Aven in 1886, he had already begun to move away from Impressionism. Looking for new forms of expression, he hoped to find in Brittany a simpler and more authentic way of life that would enable him to return to the roots of Art.

Ici, dans la
BUVETTE DE LA PLAGE,
Marie Henry
accueillit, de 1889 à 1893:
Paul Gauguin,
Jacob Meyer de Haan,
Paul Sérusier,
Charles Filiger
et
Charles Laval,
Maxime Maufra,
Emile Bernard,

At Pont-Aven he met another painter, Emile Bernard, in the boarding house run by Marie-Jeanne Gloanec where, for the next 10 years, many artists would stay and work. In 1888 Paul Sérusier

arrived in the town and the three of them became the exponents of a new style of painting, Synthétisme, in which the artist's vision took precedence over reality (their motto was 'Paint what you see, not what is there'). Experimental techniques found favour: the use of strongly contrasting colours and a return to the principles of drawing by underlining the contours of objects and figures.

Other artists joined the first three: Charles Laval, Henri Maufra, Emile

Schuffenecker, Meyer de Haan, and many others. Soon there were some 20 of them staying at the Gloanec boarding house.

In 1889 Gauguin painted the famous *Christ Jaune* (Yellow Christ) against an idyllic rural background, and *La Lutte de Jacob et de l'Ange* (Jacob Fighting the Angel), which shows that he was all the time striving for greater simplicity and becoming more daring in his compositions.

Retreat to le Pouldu

When tourists began flocking to Pont-Aven and Gauguin felt that the place was losing its original charm, he decided to move to le Pouldu, a small seaside village further south. With Laval, Filiger, and Meyer de Haan, he settled in Marie Henry's inn (*see p104*).

Gauguin's influence continued to grow, his personality dominating the other painters who, in spite of being split into two groups, became known as the School of Pont-Aven. It was not, of course, a school in the literal sense: they were simply a group of artists working and searching together for new means to transcend reality. In their search, these men became the forefathers of modern painting and of such movements as Expressionism, Surrealism, and even Abstract art.

Facing page: a plaque at the museum in Pont-Aven (above) commemorates the painters who lived at Marie Henry's inn in le Pouldu (below)
Above: Gauguin, self portrait in Breton costume

The beach at le Pouldu, the small port town where Gauguin lived after leaving Pont-Aven

Pont-l'Abbé
See p113.

Le Pouldu

Facing south, the sheltered Plage des Grands Sables is backed by high cliffs; a flight of steps climbs up to a promenade lined with hotels. Nearby stands a monument dedicated to Paul Gauguin, who spent a great deal of time in le Pouldu between 1889 and 1894. He lived with his friends in the house of Marie Henry, which they decorated profusely. The unique interior has been faithfully reconstructed in an identical house a few metres away.

The harbour is picturesquely situated at the mouth of the River Laïta, 2km away. The town is a popular horse-riding centre.

Maison Marie Henry, 10 rue des Grands Sables. Tel: 02 98 39 98 51. Open: for guided tours daily at 11am, 3.15pm, 4.15pm, 5.15pm & 6.15pm. Admission charge.

13km south of Quimperlé on the D49.

Primel-Trégastel

This resort is situated on the green hills of a narrow peninsula in a setting similar to the Côte de Granit Rose. The sandy beach stretches over 1km towards the Pointe de Primel and its striking pink rock formations. The view extends across the Bay of Morlaix to the lighthouse on the Ile de Batz.

Nearby
Le Diben

This charming fishing port specialises in shellfish stored in large seawater pools (visitors welcome). Walk to the Pointe de Diben for more enchanting views of the Bay of Morlaix.

2.5km west of Primel-Trégastel on the D46A.

St-Jean-du-Doigt

The village gets its curious name from a relic: the finger of St John the Baptist,

The fountain at St-Jean-du-Doigt shows God the Father blessing His Son's baptism by John

A quiet street in Quimperlé's upper town

supposedly brought back from the Holy Land in the 15th century. Pilgrims soon flocked to St-Jean-du-Doigt, as the relic was said to cure eye diseases. Nowadays, a *pardon* takes place in June. The parish close includes a monumental gate, a high Renaissance fountain, and an oratory.
6km southeast of Primel-Trégastel on the D46 and the D79.

Tumulus de Barnenez

Following the scenic coast road south to Morlaix, a right turn at St-Gonven takes you out on the Barnenez peninsula. There you can see a large stone mound overlooking the Bay of Morlaix, covering 11 passage graves from around 4600 BC.
12km south of Primel-Trégastel off the D76. Tel: 02 98 67 24 73.
Open: 10am–12.30pm & 2–6.30pm. Admission charge.

Quimperlé

This beautiful old town developed on an island at the confluence of the Ellé and Isole. As it grew it climbed on to the plateau, the new district was called the Ville Haute (High Town), while the medieval town became known as the Ville Basse (Low Town). The Ville Basse has retained part of its medieval character around its magnificent church. Along the rue Brémond-d'Ars are several stately stone-built houses dating from the 17th century, and nearby are the ruins of the Église St-Colomban.

Église Ste-Croix

Built at the end of the 11th century and based on Jerusalem's Church of the Holy Sepulchre, Ste-Croix was heavily restored in the 19th century when the steeple collapsed; however, the crypt and the apse are original. Note the fine arcade of the apse and the beautifully carved capitals atop the short columns of the crypt, which contains two 15th-century graves.
Rue de la Paix.

Maison des Archers

This is the best of several late medieval houses lining a narrow cobbled street. It houses a local museum devoted to the town and costumes of the region.
7 rue Dom-Morice. Tel: 02 98 96 04 32. Open: Jul & Aug 10am–noon & 2–7pm. Closed: Sun morning & Mon. Admission charge.

Nearby
La Roche du Diable

From the top of the 'Devil's Rock' there is an impressive view over the River Ellé.
12km northeast of Quimperlé on the D790 and a minor road to the right.

Quimperlé is 47km southeast of Quimper on the N165 dual carriageway.

The fine view from St-Pol-de-Léon's Kreisker chapel tower takes in the former cathedral

Roscoff

Once the hideout of notorious privateers, Roscoff is today known for the mildness of its climate, its early vegetables and exotic flowers, fine beaches and sophisticated hydrotherapy centres. It also has an important fishing fleet specialising in shellfish, and the unloading of the lobster trawlers in the old harbour is always a fascinating sight. The tiny Chapelle Ste-Barbe, built on an outcrop at the Pointe de Bloscon, overlooks the seawater pools where lobsters and crabs are stocked. Beyond lies the port of Roscoff, from which Brittany Ferries sail to Plymouth and Cork. West of the fishing harbour and marina, the rue Amiral-Réveillère, lined with fine 16th-century stone houses, leads to the church.

An abundance of flowers welcomes visitors to the offshore island of Ile de Batz (15 minutes by ferry from the port). The island is surrounded by dunes and sandy beaches, and seaweed-gathering is one of the rare traditional occupations to have survived, although today, the heavy cartloads are pulled by tractors rather than horses. The island's *école de mer* offers sea canoeing and orthodox sailing. The top of the light-house on the west side offers a good overall view.

Aquarium

Part of the Musée Océanologique is devoted to local marine flora and fauna presented in several pools that recreate their natural environment.
Place G Tessier. Tel: 02 98 29 23 25. Open: 10am–noon & 1–6pm. Admission charge.

Église Notre-Dame-de-Kroaz-Batz

This 16th-century church has a very distinctive Renaissance steeple decorated with amusing lanterns delicately carved in granite. Carvings of ships and guns on the walls are reminders of the town's privateering past. Note the 15th-century alabaster retable in the right-hand aisle.
Place Lacaze-Duthiers.

Roscoff is 25km northwest of Morlaix on the D58.

St-Pol-de-Léon

The soaring steeple of the Chapelle du Kreisker belongs to the highest belfry in Brittany and is a striking example of refined Gothic tracery. It certainly provides a very good reason to visit this compact, ancient town, one of the seven original Breton bishoprics, with its fine Norman-style cathedral containing a 10th-century sarcophagus and the relics of its founder.

St-Pol is a lively market town at the centre of a rich agricultural area. The many protected beaches invite you to relax and enjoy the view of Ile Callot and Carantec across the bay. A growing seaside resort, it also offers tennis, mini-golf, horse-riding, and cycle hire.

Nearby
The 15th-century feudal **Château de Kérouzéré** has retained only three of its machicolated corner towers. The view extends across the surrounding woods to the sea. The castle contains tapestries and Breton furniture, and the oratory is decorated with 17th-century frescoes.
8km west of St-Pol off the D10.

St-Pol-de-Léon is 20km northwest of Morlaix on the D58.

Cap Sizun
Cap Sizun's jagged promontory

offers the constant spectacle of a bitter contest between land and sea. Between the Pointe du Raz and the Ile de Sein lies the dreaded Raz de Sein, the subject of sombre shipwreck stories. A path follows the edge of the cliff to the Enfer de Plogoff, a precipice where locals claim to hear the cries of damned souls mixed with the sound of pounding waves.

Across the Baie des Trépassés, the Pointe du Van offers magnificent views of Sein and the Crozon Peninsula. Along the north coast, the dark cliffs of the Réserve du Cap Sizun are an important bird sanctuary.
Réserve du Cap Sizun.
Tel: 02 98 70 13 53. Open: mid-Mar–Jun 10am–noon & 2–6pm; Jul & Aug 10am-6pm. Admission charge.

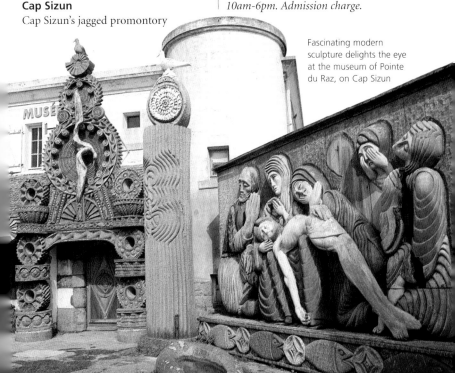

Fascinating modern sculpture delights the eye at the museum of Pointe du Raz, on Cap Sizun

Walk: Old Quimper

The oldest and most charming district of Quimper lies north of the River Odet in the vicinity of Cathédrale St-Corentin. A relaxing stroll through narrow cobbled streets will enable you to admire a fascinating variety of domestic architecture, beautifully restored timber-framed and stone houses with a wealth of interesting and often amusing carvings.

Allow 1½ hours.

Start in front of the Hôtel de Ville on the north side of the cathedral; note the strength and elegance of the flying buttresses and the elaborate porch. Follow the rue du Frout and turn right to reach the River Odet; turn right again.

1 The Town Walls

With the river on the left and a well-preserved section of the medieval town walls on the right, this part of the embankment is particularly attractive. The spires of the cathedral can be seen towering above the walls, in contrast to the red geraniums decorating the many foot-bridges spanning the Odet.

The rue du Roi Gradlon on the right leads past the Musée Départemental Breton to the place St-Corentin. Walk across the square.

2 Place St-Corentin

On your right stands the imposing cathedral, while on your left a splendid 15th-century house has been turned into a shop called L'Art de Cornouaille, which sells specialities from the region including the famous Quimper ceramics.

Follow the rue Elie Fréron up to No. 22, faced with slates. Turn back and bear right when you reach the tiny place au Beurre, where you can stop for a snack at one of the crêperies.

3 Rues du Sallé and du Guéodet

All the streets in this area are worth exploring as they contribute a great deal to the unique atmosphere of old Quimper. No. 10 rue du Sallé is particularly fine, but it is the Maison des Cariatides in the rue du Guéodet that attracts most attention, so vivid are the expressions on the faces carved below the corbel.

Turn right to return to the square and right again into the rue Kéréon.

4 Rue Kéréon

This is the high street of the old town, lined with timber-framed corbelled houses and elegant boutiques. The graceful outline of the cathedral appears at one end of the street, while at the other end a delightful view awaits you. A small bridge, formerly a drawbridge, spans the River Steir, and on the left can

be seen part of the old town wall and a picturesque *bartizan* (a projecting lookout).
Cross the bridge and turn left.

5 Place Terre-au-Duc

This was the centre of the medieval market town and is still surrounded with half-timbered houses. Nearby, the new covered market, erected in place of the old one which burned down in 1979, blends very tastefully with the old houses close to it. Walk along the quai du Port au Vin and quai du Steir, whose names may seem strange to you since there is no river in sight – but in fact, the Steir has been canalised and covered over at that point.

Turn left when you reach the embankment.

6 Rue du Parc

The wide pavement along the embankment is constantly crowded with strollers, shoppers and business people, everyone walking along at their own pace among the tables and chairs laid out in front of the attractive restaurants and cafés.

At the corner of the rue St-François, an old-fashioned shop, called Faïences de Quimper, displays colourful specimens of the famous local ceramics. *A little further on the left, the rue du Roi Gradlon takes you back to the place St-Corentin and the Hôtel de Ville.*

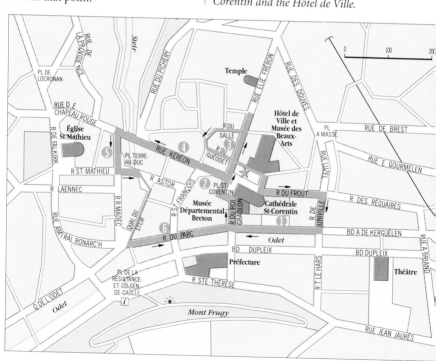

By Bike: The Crozon Peninsula

These two cycle tours take in the scenic countryside at the extremity of the Crozon Peninsula, an area of wild beauty now included in the Parc Naturel Régional d'Armorique.

TOUR 1
This 38-km tour, which takes about half a day, explores the northern part of Crozon around Camaret-sur-Mer.

1 Camaret-sur-Mer
This lively seaside resort and fishing port, specialising in lobster, occupies a sheltered position inside a tiny cove formed by the Sillon de Camaret. The fort built by Vauban at the tip of this sandbank is a reminder that Camaret once guarded the entrance to Brest roadstead and was often attacked by

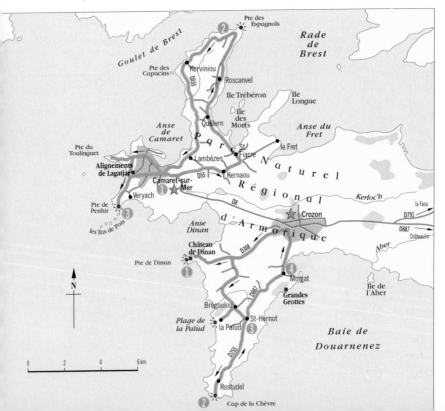

English, Spanish, and Dutch ships.
Follow the D55 east to St-Fiacre, turn left on the D355, and continue along the road that closely follows the coast to the Pointe des Espagnols.

2 Pointe des Espagnols

Overlooking the entrance of the Brest road, the point gets its name from a fort built there by Spanish troops to blockade Brest in support of the Catholic cause during the 16th-century Wars of Religion. The fort was later razed to the ground. The view extends over Brest, the Elorn estuary spanned by an elegant bridge and the Plougastel peninsula.
The road skirts the strait known as the Goulet de Brest, then turns south towards Camaret. Continue west to the Pointe du Toulinguet; your next stop is the famous Pointe de Penhir. Turn back, then right at the first opportunity.

3 Pointe de Penhir

Just outside Camaret you will pass a group of megaliths (*see pp124–5*) known as the **Alignements de Lagatjar**. These consist of three rows of standing stones – over 140 in all – most of which had fallen and were raised again in the 1930s. Seen from the top of the 70-m high cliff there is a sheer drop to dark jagged rocks and the famous **Tas de Pois**, pyramid-shaped reefs, sticking out of the steel-grey ocean. A monument honours the Free French forces of World War II.
Return to Camaret.

TOUR 2

Although less spectacular, this 30-km tour of the southern Crozon Peninsula

gives a good overall impression of this heath-covered area. *Allow half a day.*

Start from the modern resort of Crozon; follow the D308 to the Pointe de Dinan.

1 Pointe de Dinan

Apart from the view, the attraction here is the Château de Dinan, a huge rock looking like a ruined castle and linked to the main part of the cliff by a natural arch; this 'drawbridge' gives access for those who wish to explore further.
Turn back, then head south towards Cap de la Chèvre. The Plage de la Palud on the right is dangerous, but it offers close-up views of the rocky coastline.

2 Cap de la Chèvre

Views extend over the whole length of Cap Sizun prolonged by the Ile de Sein. A former German observation post stands at the furthest point.
Turn back.

3 St-Hernot

Housed in the old village school, the **Maison des Minéraux** exhibits more than 500 minerals from all over Brittany and explains the geology of the region.
Continue to Morgat.

4 Morgat

Morgat has a kind of old-world charm when it was a fashionable resort. Today, its sheltered beach draws many families, while the plentiful local fishing grounds are popular with fishing enthusiasts. Several interesting caves south of the promontory known as Beg ar Gador can be visited by boat from the harbour.
Return to Crozon.

Tour: In the Painters' Footsteps

During the 19th century, several groups of painters 'discovered' Brittany, and it was their enthusiasm that gave birth to a great variety of conventional and modern works. Quite a few of these artists were seduced by the remote region of Cornouaille, its unspoilt landscapes, its unaffected people, and the harmony between man and nature. This 100-km long tour takes you through Bigouden country.

Allow a whole day.

Start from Quimper and visit the Musée des Beaux-Arts with its fine collection of 19th- and 20th-century paintings of Breton inspiration. Drive south to Bénodet then cross the River Odet.

1 Ste-Marine

Facing Bénodet across the river, the

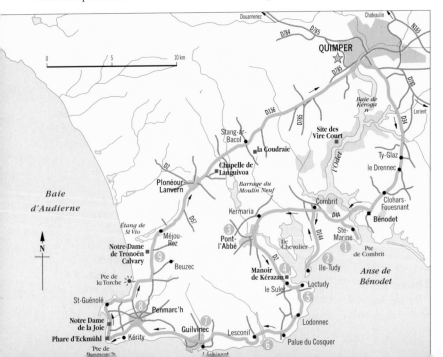

village centre forms a charming setting with its church and tiny harbour. *Drive back to the main road, turn left, then left again on the D144.*

2 Ile-Tudy

In spite of its name, Ile-Tudy is no longer an island. Facing Loctudy across a narrow strait, it is an attractive traditional seaside village with narrow streets, low houses and a vast beach. *Return to the main road, turn left.*

3 Pont-l'Abbé

The castle keep houses the Musée Bigouden containing furniture, handicrafts, costumes, and headdresses typical of the area. On the way to Loctudy, 2km out of town, the Maison du Pays Bigouden is a traditional farm illustrating daily life at the end of the19th century, when the painters lived around here. *Continue on the D2.*

4 Manoir de Kérazan

The refined interior of this elegant manor house enhances a fine collection of paintings, the majority of which are connected with Brittany and Breton life.

5 Loctudy

This peaceful family resort is one of the busiest fishing ports on the south coast, with a splendid church. It seems as if nothing has changed in a hundred years. *Drive west and turn left on the D102.*

6 Lesconil

Lined with restaurants and typical Breton houses, the fishing harbour is particularly charming, livening up

between 5pm and 6pm when the *malamoks* (small wooden trawlers) come back with the day's catch. *Drive west along the coast.*

7 Le Guilvinec

The fourth most important fishing port in France, le Guilvinec specialises in local fishing for some 60 different varieties of fish. *Continue to Penmarc'h.*

8 Penmarc'h and St-Guénolé

The whole area around Penmarc'h inspired several generations of painters including Lemordant, whose work can be seen in the Musée des Beaux-Arts in Quimper. Look at the Église St-Nonna in Penmarc'h before moving on to the Pointe de Penmarc'h. Slightly north, St-Guénolé is famous for its rocky shoreline. *Drive north, keeping as close to the coast as possible.*

9 Notre-dame de Tronoën Calvary

Set among sand dunes close to the sea, this is one of the oldest of Brittany's great calvaries, dating from the mid-15th century. An important *pardon* takes place here in September. *Return to Quimper via Plonéour-Lanvern.*

Manoir de Kérazan *Tel: 02 98 87 40 40.* Open: Jun–Aug 10.30am–7pm. Closed: Tue. Admission charge.
Maison du Pays Bigouden *Tel: 02 98 87 35 63.* Open: Jun–Sep 10am–12.30pm & 3–6.30pm. Closed: Sun. Admission charge.
Musée Bigouden *Tel: 02 98 66 09 09.* Open: Jun–Sep 9am–noon & 2–6pm. Closed: Thu. Admission charge.

Southern Brittany

Although here the battle between land and sea is a thing of the past, it has nevertheless left its mark. The coastal area is indented by deep, wide estuaries and the vast expanse of the Golfe du Morbihan (now offering the safest bathing and sailing facilities in Brittany), while the fascinating marshland of the Grande Brière and the salt marshes of the Guérande peninsula near la Baule were created by sand deposits.

The Venus of Quinipily, Baud: formerly an object of veneration in defiance of church authorities

One might be tempted to say that in southern Brittany everything happens along the coast, just as northern Brittany's life is organised round its busy Channel ports and resorts. Although not an entirely accurate description, it is true to say that southern Brittany's pulse is powered by its sunny shoreline.

Brittany's 'Gentle' Coastline

The word 'gentle' used to describe part of Brittany's coast might seem exaggerated. Yet, compared to the spectacular cliffs of the Côte d'Emeraude or the austere west coast round Cap Sizun and the Crozon Peninsula, the south coast appears definitely smoother and tamer – allowing a few exceptions like the Côte Sauvage of the Quiberon Peninsula.

'Gentle' also because of its particularly mild and sunny climate, the south coast attracts crowds of holiday-makers to its fashionable beaches at Quiberon and la Baule ('the Nice of the North').

But there are idyllic beaches all along the coast, so those who prefer a more peaceful environment will find a wide choice, in particular between the Rhuys Peninsula and the Pointe du Croisic west of La Baule.

Another aspect of the area's attractions are its islands, many of which can be reached by scheduled boat trips. Ile de Groix and above all Belle-Ile, the largest island off the coast of Brittany, are well worth a visit.

Rivers and Old Towns

Several rivers – such as the Erdre, the Vilaine, the Blavet and their tributaries – wind their way towards the south coast through green countryside and tracts of forest like the Landes de Lanvaux.

The Nantes-Brest Canal, running from east to west, links the Erdre, the Vilaine, the Oust, and the Blavet, completing an extensive network of waterways that appeals to river-cruising enthusiasts.

South of the canal, many towns retain their ancient character and a wealth of varied, well-preserved domestic architecture. Among them is Vannes, the capital of Morbihan; the walled town of Guérande; Rochefort-en-Terre, famous for its stone houses; and the riverside towns of Malestroit, Pontivy and Auray.

Southern Brittany also has some impressive examples of military architecture, including the splendid feudal castle at Josselin and the dramatic ruins of the Château de Suscinio overlooking the sea.

Heritage of Mystery and Beauty

Just as Finistère is famous for its calvaries and parish closes, southern Brittany is famous for its megaliths, and in particular the *alignements* at Carnac.

Much has been written about these long rows of granite standing stones, but after several thousand years they remain mysterious (*see pp124–5*). However, massive, rude of shape, and undeniably a major feature of the landscape where they exist, they in no way overshadow the refined beauty found elsewhere in the region in such artistic treasures as St-Fiacre Chapel, near le Faouët to the west.

Southern Brittany

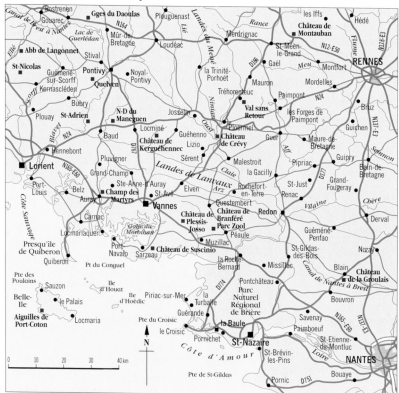

Nantes

Officially the capital of the Loire region but Breton at heart, Nantes lies at the confluence of the Loire and the Erdre, rivers that are now mostly canalised. The city followed the ups and downs of its maritime trade, until the creation of the port of St-Nazaire and the dredging of the Loire estuary enabled it to expand its industrial activities. Nantes is now the economic metropolis of western France.

Passage Pommeraye: shop till you drop, in style

Brittany's Former Capital

Nantes was Brittany's first capital in the 10th century, but throughout the Middle Ages it was in bitter competition with Rennes for the privilege. The city's golden age came in the 15th century, when both the cathedral and the castle were built by the Dukes of Brittany. Nantes finally conceded its rival's supremacy when the Breton Parliament based itself in Rennes after the Act of Union with France was signed in 1532. It was briefly the focus of attention again in 1598, when Henri IV signed the famous Edict of Nantes establishing religious freedom throughout the kingdom.

No longer a seat of political power, Nantes achieved economic supremacy through the sugar and slave trade. The abolition of the slave trade, the turbulence of the Revolution and a drop in the import of sugar cane put an end to this prosperity, and Nantes had to turn to industrial activities, acquiring a new port at the entrance of the Loire estuary that could accommodate large ships.

The various stages of the town's development are still apparent today. The 19th-century district is separated from the medieval town by the cours des 50 Otages (one of modern Nantes' main arteries), while south of the cours Franklin-Roosevelt the Ile Feydeau is an enclave of 18th-century elegance at the heart of the city. Striking modern buildings near the river form part of an ambitious town-planning programme and testify to Nantes's new vitality. (For a tour of the medieval town, *see pp134–5*.)

Medieval architecture of Nantes

Nantes

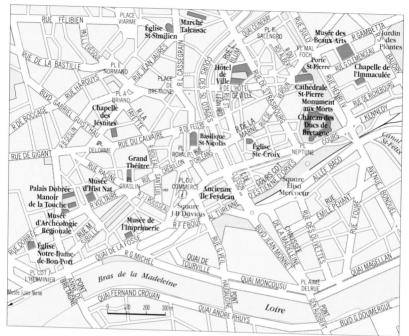

Château des Ducs de Bretagne

Built in the 15th century by Duke François II and his daughter Anne on the banks of the Loire, the castle received many distinguished guests. After being used as a garrison for 200 years, it has found a new cultural vocation as a museum complex.

Surrounded by thick walls and a moat, four buildings dating from different periods face the inner court-yard. The two original ones are the Dukes' living quarters, known as the Grand Logis and the Grand Gouvernement or Official Palace (the latter now houses a Musée Régional des Arts Populaires containing typical Breton furniture, costumes, and crafts). The Petit Gouvernement is Renaissance in style, and the largest building, called Harnachement, dates from the 18th century; it houses the Musée des Salorges, devoted primarily to the town's maritime history.

1 place Marc Elder. Tel: 02 40 41 56 56.
Open: Jul & Aug 10am–noon & 2–6pm.
Closed: Tue, Sep–Jun.
Admission charge (free on Sun).

Nantes is 385km southwest of Paris on the A11 motorway, 108km south of Rennes on the N137 dual carriageway. It is 2 hours from Paris by TGV (fast train). The Nantes/Atlantique International Airport, 10km to the south, is directly linked to Paris, London and other European main towns.
Office de Tourisme: place Saint Pierre.
Tel: 02 40 20 60 000. Open: daily 10am–1pm, 2–6pm.

Ile Feydeau

This boat-shaped piece of land was still an island in the River Loire when a series of beautiful stone residences were built on it by the city's wealthiest merchants during the 18th century. The façades are decorated with *mascarons* (stone masks, often of mythological characters) and with corbelled balconies. Walk along the Allée de Turenne and admire Nos 3, 8, 9, 10, 11, and 13, then rue Kervégan where Nos 9, 18, and 30 are particularly interesting, and finally Allée Duguay-Trouin, to see Nos 8, 9, 10, 15, and 16.

Musée des Beaux-Arts

This is one of France's main regional fine arts museums, with collections covering seven centuries of international art. The major European schools are represented with masterpieces by Tintoretto, Rubens, Georges de la Tour, Watteau, and others. The rich collection of French 19th-century paintings includes works by Delacroix, Courbet, and Corot, while 20th-century art is represented by Monet, Max Ernst, Chagall, Kandinsky, Picasso, and Tinguely.
10 rue Georges Clemenceau. Tel: 02 40 41 65 65. Open: Mon, Wed, Thu, Sat & Sun 10am–6pm, Fri 10am–8pm. Closed: Tue. Admission charge.

Musées Départementaux

These County Museums are housed in three neighbouring buildings: the Palais Dobrée, dating from the 19th century; the 15th-century Manoir de la Touche, the former country residence of the Bishops of Nantes; and a building of recent construction. Donated to the *département* by a rich shipowner, the Musée Thomas Dobrée contains his personal collections including rare illuminated manuscripts and books, engravings, alabaster objects, paintings, tapestries, ceramics, jewels, arms, and ivories. The Musée d'Archéologie Régionale presents regional prehistory and history up to the Renaissance period, illustrated mainly through local archaeological finds.
18 Rue Voltaire. Tel: 02 40 71 03 50. Open: 9.45am–5.30pm. Closed: Mon. Admission charge (free on Sun).

Musée d'Histoire Naturelle

Considered one of the most beautiful in France, this museum has extensive collections of zoology, palaeontology, mineralogy and ethnography. An area called Espace Science Nature has been specially designed for children from four to 14 years old.
12 rue Voltaire. Tel: 02 40 41 67 67. Open: 10–11.45am & 2–5.45pm. Closed: Sun morning & Mon. Admission charge (free on Sun).

Musée Jules Verne

Devoted to the science fiction writer born in Nantes in 1828, this museum contains mementoes as well as books, posters, photographs, and objects that illustrate the imaginary world he created.
3 rue de l'Hermitage. Tel: 02 40 69 72 52. Open: 10am–noon & 2–6pm. Closed: Sun morning & Tue. Admission charge (free on Sun).

The 19th-century District

The wealth and style of an earlier era are still evident west of the cours des 50

Otages. In the centre of the place Royale stands a handsome fountain erected in 1865 depicting Nantes, the river Loire and its tributaries.

Leading off it is the rue Crébillon, a busy shopping street so popular with the locals that they have invented the verb *crébillonner* to describe their favourite pastime! Halfway down on the left is the entrance of the passage Pommeraye, an opulent triple-tiered shopping gallery created in 1843.

The regal, 18th-century Grand Théâtre stands on the place Graslin, which formed the nucleus of development at the beginning of the 19th century. To the southwest, the cours Cambronne, lined with stately residences, offers a glimpse of the Loire in the distance. On the north side of the rue Voltaire, several museums stand close to one another.

Parks and Gardens

The landscaped Jardin des Plantes boasts camellias, magnolias, and rhododendrons as well as collections of rare plants, some of them in hothouses. The Ile de Versailles in the River Erdre has a lovely Japanese garden with picturesque rockeries and cascading streams. Northwest of the town centre, the Parc de Procé is a 16-hectare English-style park with a children's area: access is via rue de la Bastille and rue des Dervallièr.

Château des Ducs: scene of Anne's marriage to Louis XII and the signing of the Edict of Nantes

Auray

The name of this sleepy town on the banks of the peaceful River Loch is familiar to all Bretons because of its famous historical and religious associations. The Battle of Auray – which in 1364 ended the War of Succession, one of the bloodiest events in Brittany's history – took place just north of the city in the Marais de Kerzo.

The Bretons had mixed feelings about the outcome. They mourned the death of the French pretender, Charles de Blois, who was later canonised, and they resented the fact that Jean de Montfort won the battle with the help of the English. But Montfort proved to be a good Duke, and under his leadership Brittany entered a period of stability and prosperity. All things considered, they forgave Montfort, especially since he commissioned the building of a chapel on the spot where his rival fell. Known as the Chartreuse d'Auray, the church stands next to a funeral chapel built in the 19th century as a memorial to royalists and Chouans shot in 1795.

St-Goustan

Enclosed within a bend of the River Loch and linked to the rest of the town by an old stone bridge, this is a very pretty district, with its steep narrow streets lined with 15th-century houses.

From the place St-Sauveur by the bridge, walk round to the quai Benjamin-Franklin. The name is a reminder that, over 200 years ago, the famous American politician/inventor paid an unexpected visit to Auray, landing here when he came to negotiate a treaty with France against the English during the American War of Independence; look at the plaque on the wall of No. 8. The Promenade du Loch on the opposite bank occupies the site of the castle which was razed to the ground in 1558.

The tiny river port of St-Goustan, favourite subject of artists, where Benjamin Franklin lived

La Baule is popular for its modern salt-water cures as well as its grand beach and casino

Ste-Anne-d'Auray

One of the most famous *pardons*, dedicated to the patron saint of Brittany, takes place on 26th July in this village north of Auray. It all started in 1625 when, following a revelation, a humble farmer found an ancient statue of St Anne, mother of the Virgin Mary, buried in one of his fields. A church was built almost immediately, although it was replaced by the present basilica in the 19th century.
6km north on the D17.

Auray is 22km west of Vannes on the N165.

Baud

Lying at the heart of typical Breton countryside, in the green Blavet valley on the edge of the Camors Forest, this small town is famous for the unusual Vénus de Quinipily. The statue's pagan origins caused it to be thrown into the River Blavet several times by Church authorities, where it became quite battered. The Lord of the Manor ordered a copy to be made and it is this that now stands on top of the fountain in a lovely rural setting (the original is long since lost). The place is the

rendezvous of modern Druids, and with lucky timing you might catch one of their religious ceremonies.
Vénus de Quinipily, 2km southwest on the D724 to Hennebont.

St-Adrien

This tiny granite village has a lovely 15th-century chapel, surrounded by fountains which are said to have healing powers.
6km northwest of le Baud on a minor road.

Baud is 35km northwest of Vannes on the D779.

La Baule

At the heart of the Côte d'Amour (Love Coast), an intriguing name in itself, la Baule became a fashionable resort during the second half of the 19th century and has since acquired international fame. The beautiful beach alone is worth a detour, as very few anywhere combine so many positive features. Its 7-km long stretch of golden sand follows the smooth curve of a well-sheltered south-facing bay, backed by splendid villas, luxury hotels and apartments, hydrotherapy centres, and a casino.

Le Pouliguen and Pornichet

Adjacent to la Baule are two smaller resorts. Le Pouliguen, meaning 'small white cove' in Breton, was the first to be launched when this part of the coast was still a succession of shifting dunes. Pornichet, formerly a salt-marsh workers' village, now shares its marina with la Baule.

La Baule is 17km west of St-Nazaire on the D92.

Belle-Ile

As well as being the largest island off the coast of Brittany (17km long), Belle-Ile is also the most beautiful. Even great artists like Claude Monet were inspired by its scenery. During the 18th century, a few hundred Canadians settled on Belle-Ile; no ordinary immigrants, they were of French descent and had voluntarily left their native Canada after it officially became a British colony. From the New World they brought back the potato!

Because of its strategic position close to the Loire estuary, Belle-Ile was attacked many times by the Dutch and English fleets and was twice occupied by the English. For a while it belonged to Nicolas Fouquet, Louis XIV's ambitious finance minister, who spared no expense in fortifying the island. The island's backbone is a schistose plateau, itself treeless, cut by green valleys running down to the coast and leading to tiny beaches and small natural harbours. The sheltered east coast provides numerous bathing facilities, while the west coast, known as the Côte Sauvage, offers ruggedly beautiful scenery.

Belle-Ile is well equipped to receive tourists, with several large hotels and a golf course overlooking the sea. The farming population lives in four villages and many hamlets spread about the island.

Le Palais

This small harbour centred on the northeast coast, facing the mainland, is Belle-Ile's administrative and commercial centre and the gateway to the island, as the defensive citadel guarding its entrance testifies. In 1650 Fouquet had the original structure, a 16th-century castle, extended and strengthened by Vauban, Louis XIV's master of military architecture.

Locmaria

Set along the eastern edge of Belle-Ile, the village has a charming church called Notre-Dame de Boistord, which is linked to a strange legend: when Dutch sailors felled a splendid elm growing in front of the church to replace their broken mast, the tree became all twisted and useless, and the terrified sailors ran away!

Sauzon

This seaside village has one of the most popular marinas on Brittany's south coast, and a golf course beckons nearby.

Aiguilles de Port-Coton

This group of reefs off the Côte Sauvage, showing above the foamy Atlantic, was painted 38 times by Claude Monet.

Access by boat from Quiberon (tel: 02 97 31 80 01), crossing 20–45 minutes, or by air from Lorient and Quiberon (tel: 02 97 31 41 14).

Carnac

This is a pleasant, unpretentious little resort in its own right, with curving, gently shelving beaches. But, with its unique concentration of megaliths, Carnac is known mainly as the capital of prehistoric Brittany.

Megaliths

Situated north of the village, the menhirs are arranged mainly in three lots of *alignements*, the most impressive

being the **Alignements du Ménec**.
Once hidden by dense forest, the Ménec *alignement* is over 1-km long and comprises more than a thousand standing stones. Some of these are arranged in a half or full circle, termed a cromlech. Closer to the village, the Tumulus St-Michel is a stone and earth mound covering several funeral chambers; some of the objects found inside are exhibited in the Prehistory Museum. There are other megaliths all around the area; some can be spotted in old stone walls bordering farmers' fields!
Tumulus St-Michel. Currently visits are not allowed for security reasons.

Musée de la Préhistoire
The museum's collections – the third largest in Europe – cover a huge span of time from the palaeolithic era to the early Middle Ages.
Tel: 02 97 52 22 04. Open: Jun–Sep 10am–6.30pm, rest of the year 10am–noon & 2–5pm. Closed: Tue. Admission charge.

Nearby
La Trinité-sur-Mer
A popular seaside resort and yachting centre with several fine beaches and a lively marina. There is a lovely overall view from the Pont de Kerisper over the harbour and the River Crach.
5km east of Carnac on the D781.

Carnac is 34km southeast of Lorient on the D781.

The massive granite *alignements* in Carnac: so purposefully arranged, so unfathomably obscure

Megaliths

The astonishing concentration and variety of megaliths found in Brittany, particularly along the south coast, never cease to fascinate archaeologists, who are striving to solve the mystery of these granite monuments erected between 5000 and 2000 BC.

Deceptively simple in concept, yet with a profound visual impact, they are our only link with a civilisation about which we know very little. But as an indelible mark on the land, these are among the oldest existing examples of stone architecture, one of the first cultural achievements of Neolithic man, whose genius reached its apex with the construction of the Egyptian pyramids.

A World Fit for Giants

These monuments were called megaliths because they were literally 'large stones' – so large, in fact, that they entered the imaginary world of Breton legend as being the work of giants or fairies. Hence the name la Roche aux Fées, given to one of the finest passage graves in Brittany, made up of 40 huge blocks of purple schist (*see p43*).

The erection of the megaliths – weighing up to 45 tons – implied the use of a large workforce and, consequently, the presence of elaborate social structures able to organise this extraordinary collective enterprise.

A Stone Heritage

As megaliths are particularly plentiful in Brittany, the words used to designate the different types were borrowed from the Breton language during the 18th century.

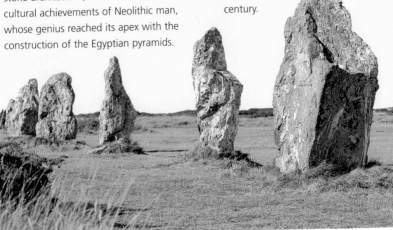

Menhir, for instance, comes from *men* (stone) and *hir* (long). There are more than 5,000 of these standing stones in Brittany, either isolated or in groups like the *alignements,* or the semi-circular or circular *cromlechs.* Heights and shapes vary a great deal.

Dolmens ('stone tables' in Breton) consist of large slabs mounted on upright stones. Sometimes decorated with engravings, they can be preceded by a corridor, or buried under a stone or earth mound with access through a covered passage, in which case the

whole is called a tumulus. The most famous is the Tumulus de Barnenez near Morlaix.

The Mystery Remains

Experts have long debated the purpose of megaliths. Everyone more or less agrees that they are somehow connected with religious practices, but a lot of questions remain unanswered. For example, there is no doubt that dolmens are graves, but whose? As for menhirs, they are even more difficult to interpret. Were they land-marks? Signposts? Were they linked to some kind of astronomical study? Will they – can they – ever yield the answer to their mystery?

Facing page above: Allée Couverte, Ile Grande; below: Alignement de Lagatjar, Crozon Peninsula
This page: Dolmen des Pierres Plates (above); Table des Merchands, Locmariaquer (below)

The busy port of Le Croisic

Le Croisic

This photogenic resort offers holiday-makers two very different beaches – the sheltered St-Goustan, and Port-Lin, exposed to the bracing ocean breeze – as well as a fishing harbour and marina situated inside the laguna near the salt marshes. Seventeenth-century houses decorated with wrought-iron balconies line the quayside, with more old houses in the vicinity of the church. For good overall views, climb the tower on top of the man-made Mont-Esprit. A scenic road follows the Côte Sauvage from Le Croisic right round to la Baule.

Océarium

A transparent tunnel leads right across the bottom of a giant tank, with fish swimming above and beside you. A room near the entrance shows a film about salt-farming in the nearby marshes.
Ave de St-Goustan. Tel: 02 40 23 02 44.
Open: Jun–Aug 10am–7pm (closes 6pm & for lunch rest of the year).
Admission charge.

Le Croisic is 10km west of la Baule on the N171.

Le Faouët

You won't be able to resist the impressive covered market on the large village square. The ambience is magnetic and the restaurants and crêperies inviting. Once refreshed, you'll feel up to the aesthetic experience that awaits you when you visit the Chapelle St-Fiacre just outside the town.

Chapelle St-Fiacre

This interesting chapel is a gem of Flamboyant Gothic architecture, both outside and inside. Its originality lies in the asymmetry of the plain façade, with its elegant belltower and two slim turrets linked by a corbelled platform. The real treat, however, awaits you inside, where you are met by the magnificent painted rood screen, an outstanding masterpiece of intricate carving illlustrating the crucified Christ between the two thieves, but also many popular scenes, with angels on the nave side and animals on the choir side.

Christian and Celtic symbolism abounds: instructive biblical scenes are on the nave side, where the moon suggests the darkness of ignorance, and representations of the Seven Deadly Sins face the choir side, where the sun symbolises enlightenment and knowledge. Notice also the fine stained glass in the chancel.
2.5km south on the D790.

Nearby
Chapelle Ste-Barbe

The setting here is most surprising, with an elaborate 17th-century pilgrims' stairway leading down a rocky escarpment to the Flamboyant Gothic

chapel, contrasting greatly with the natural landscape all round. Inside, notice the stone vaulting (rare in Brittany) and the splendid Renaissance stained-glass windows.
3km northeast of le Faouët.

Le Faouët is 21km northeast of Quimperlé on the D790.

La Grande Brière
See p146.

Guérande

With its medieval contours, the walled town of Guérande stands on a plateau overlooking salt marshes. The *boulevard périphérique* offers a close-up view of the well-preserved fortifications dating from the 14th and 15th centuries, which include four gates leading into the town.

The most imposing is the Porte St-Michel (also called the Château, since it was the governor's official residence); it now houses an interesting local museum. Converging streets lead from the gates to the city centre and the mainly Gothic Collégiale St-Aubin, with its outside pulpit, carved capitals in the nave and 6th-century sarcophagus in a side chapel.
Museum tel: 02 40 42 96 52.
Open: Easter–Sep 10am–12.30pm & 2.30–7pm. Admission charge.

9km north of la Baule on the D92.

Salt Marshes
From the air these shallow adjoining basins of sea water look like a huge puzzle . As the water evaporates, it leaves behind a white deposit: natural sea salt. Keep a sharp eye out and you might spot a *paludier* (salt-marsh worker) gathering the precious salt with a long traditional rake. The small white mounds, reflected in the water, are a familiar sight round Saillé, where the Maison des Paludiers illustrates the life and work of salt-marsh workers. Roadside stalls in the area sell freshly gathered salt in small bags. Guided tours of salt marshes by appointment (*tel: 02 40 62 21 96*).

The Chapelle Ste-Barbe near le Faouët, with a model ship and finely carved lords' gallery

Hennebont

This ancient medieval town, one of the most heavily fortified river ports of the Middle Ages, is set on the banks of the Blavet. Today it is famous for its fishing and for its stud farm (*haras*) established in 1987 and open to the public. The late Gothic Église Notre-Dame-du-Paradis has a massive west tower with several pinnacles; it overlooks the walled town accessible through the imposing Porte Broërec. From the rampart walk there are views of the Blavet valley.
For haras *details, tel: 02 97 89 40 30.*

Hennebont is 10km northeast of Lorient.

Josselin

The highlight of this charming little town is Brittany's most prestigious château, reflected in the still waters of the River Oust. At the foot of the castle, a small mooring welcomes river-cruising visitors travelling the Nantes-Brest Canal. The nearby Pont Ste-Croix offers striking views of its tall towers. The friendly little square in front of the church invites you to sit a while outside one of the cafés, while taking in the winding cobbled streets and half-timbered buildings of Josselin, some 14th-century.

Château

Closely associated with the powerful Rohan family (who still own it), the castle was twice dismantled, but each time rose again. A fairy-tale mixture of military and domestic architecture set in a small park, it still has four of its original nine lofty towers; the living quarters are elaborated with carved pinnacles, gables, dormer windows, and balustrades. In the former stables, the **Musée des Poupées** contains several hundred dolls and dolls' furniture from all over the world.
Tel: 02 97 22 36 45. Open: Jul & Aug 10am–6pm; Jun & Sep 2–6pm. Admission charge.

The proud castle of Josselin has elaborate granite carvings overlooking its courtyard

A regal setting for the Virgin in her chapel in Josselin's Église Notre-Dame-du-Roncier

Église Notre-Dame-du-Roncier

The late Gothic church is said to stand on the spot where, around AD 800, a farmer discovered a statue of the Virgin Mary under a bramble bush (*roncier* in French). An important *pardon* takes place in September.

Nearby

In the tiny village of **Guéhenno** stands a famous calvary dating from 1550.
11km southwest of Josselin on the D126 and D123.

Josselin is 40km northeast of Vannes on the D126.

Kernascléden

Notre-Dame de Kernascléden is one of the most beautiful churches in rural Brittany; legend says that it was built at the same time as St-Fiacre chapel, 15km away, with angels carrying the same tools back and forth! The elegant steeple and the graceful pinnacles contrast with the austere granite of the building. Notice the statues of the Twelve Apostles decorating the south porch. Inside are some remarkable 15th-century frescoes.
15km east of le Faouët on the D782.

Lorient

This town gets its name from the Far Eastern trade on which it was founded. The Compagnie des Indes has long since disappeared, but the town has developed its industry and commerce and is today France's second largest fishing port and a major naval base. Almost entirely rebuilt since World War II, Lorient's appeal lies in the annual Festival Interceltique in August. A morning tour of the colourful, bustling fishing harbour of Kéroman is also strongly recommended. There is a daily 45-minute boat service to the Ile de Groix, which has a bird sanctuary and offers sandy beaches, sailing, skin-diving, and horse-riding between menhirs.

Citadelle Port-Louis

Named after Louis XIII, the stark and functional-looking citadel was built by military architect Vauban for Richelieu, incorporating previous Spanish fortifications; it was later used as a prison. Climb on top of the walls for an overall view of the town and across to Lorient. The citadel houses several museums including the Musée de la Compagnie des Indes.
Tel: 02 97 12 10 37. Open: Apr–Sep 10am–6.30pm. Closed: Tue. Admission charge.

Lorient is 50km west of Vannes on the N165 dual carriageway.

Golfe du Morbihan

Morbihan means 'little sea' in Breton, and this is exactly what the Gulf of Morbihan is: an almost enclosed expanse of water with countless islands and a rich, unique ecosystem. At low tide, fishing and pleasure boats sit stranded on its mudflats.

The best way to explore the Gulf is by boat. If you have your own or can hire one, you will discover many small harbours and moorings along the indented coastline. If not, there are regular boat trips from Vannes, Port-Navalo, Locmariaquer, and Auray. You can also walk round the Gulf along a network of paths that hug the shore.

The Islands

Three islands in the Gulf are well worth a visit. The **Ile d'Arz**, reached from Vannes, has beautiful beaches, a sailing school, and succulent oysters. Boats at Port-Blanc or Locmariaquer go to the **Ile aux Moines**, the largest of all the islands, with its delightful cottages, dolmens across the heath, and exotic plants. On the **Ile de Gavrinis**, close to Larmor-Baden, there is a famous prehistoric cairn over a passage grave (possibly that of a Druid chieftain) with upright supports covered in carvings. *Gavrinis Tumulus tel: 02 97 57 19 38. Open: Mar–Oct for guided tours only (phone for times). Admission charge.*

Little Port-Navalo, on the tip of the Rhuys Peninsula, stands at the entrance to the Gulf

Ploërmel's church portals depict scenes both sacred and secular

Locmariaquer

A number of megaliths can be found in and around this village situated at the entrance of the Gulf. The most interesting is the Grand Menhir Brisé, broken into four pieces, totalling over 20m in length and weighing 350 tons. Nearby, the Table des Marchand is an imposing passage grave decorated with carvings.

Megaliths – off the D781. Tel: 02 97 57 37 59. Open: all year round though hours vary. Guided tours. Admission charge.

Rhuys Peninsula

This curving peninsula all but closes off the southern end of the Golfe du Morbihan. Just before you reach the narrow extremity, notice the Tumulus de Tumiac, also known as 'Caesar's Mound', because from that vantage point the Roman leader is said to have watched his (rowed) war galleys defeat the becalmed sailing fleet of the local Veneti, a battle that decided the fate of Brittany. He couldn't have chosen a better place, as the view takes in not only the Gulf but also Quiberon Bay and the islands of Houat and Hoëdic in the distance. A little further on, the seaside resort of Port-Navalo has a regular boat service across the strait to Locmariaquer.

Along the Atlantic side are the imposing ruins of the Château de Suscinio (*see p139*) and the peaceful village of St-Gildas-de-Rhuys, where for a short while the ancient monastery had Abélard as its abbot, after he was brutally castrated by the Parisian guardian of Héloïse. The old abbey church has a Romanesque chancel; St-Gildas' tomb lies behind the main altar.

Ploërmel

Ploërmel lies at the heart of a varied rural area, between the Forest of Paimpont and the Landes de Lanvaux, close to the Nantes-Brest Canal and the picturesque towns of Josselin and Malestroit. During the War of Succession in 1351, the town was occupied by the English while Josselin was held by the French. As neither side was getting anywhere, it was decided that 30 knights from each side would fight it out halfway between the two towns (a column marks the place today). Josselin's knights won the epic battle, which went down in history as the Combat des Trente.

The Gothic-Renaissance Église St-Armel has a beautiful north porch with twin portals and lovely stained-glass windows. Nearby are some fine old houses, in particular the Maison des Marmousets in the rue de Beaumanoir, opposite the former residence of the Dukes of Brittany.

46km northeast of Vannes on the N166.

La Roche-Bernard: the suspension bridge, built in 1960, is over 50m above the Vilaine

Pontivy

Pontivy is a town with a split persona-lity. To the north lies the medieval town, dominated by the defensive Rohan castle and its dry moat. You can admire its timber-framed houses by wandering through the narrow streets round the place du Martray and the rues du Fil, du Perroquet and du Pont.

Southward lies the military town created by Napoléon in 1805, a pleasing mix of boulevards, administrative buildings, barracks, and landscaped squares. To avoid confronting the British navy on the coast, the lower Blavet was canalised and construction begun on a canal between the major ports of Nantes and Brest. Pontivy is a good base from which to visit the Blavet valley to the south, near the Site de Castennec.
Château de Pontivy tel: 02 97 25 12 93. Open: Jul–Sep 10.30am–7pm. Admission charge.

Nearby

The steeple of the 15th-century **Notre-Dame de Quelven** can be spotted from afar. The imposing building stands on the village square, its tower and porch decorated with fine Gothic tracery. A statue of the Virgin and Child opens to reveal 12 panels depicting the life of Christ. Nearby there is a picturesque fountain. There is a *pardon* in August. *10km southwest of Pontivy on the D2.*

Pontivy is 50km north of Vannes on the D767.

Presqu'île de Quiberon

The Quiberon Peninsula, formerly an island, is joined to the mainland by a narrow strip of sand dunes planted with pine trees. Sea and wind have shaped the land. The sheltered eastern coast is lined with beaches, while the Atlantic side is rightly known as the Côte Sauvage for the wild beauty of its cliffs, rock formations, and tiny coves where bathing is strictly forbidden. Facing south, the main resort of Quiberon has a fine beach, a renowned hydrotherapy centre, and a daily boat service to the islands of Belle-Ile, Houat, and Hoëdic. At the height of the holiday season, cars crowd the D768 down the peninsula.

La Roche-Bernard

This once busy commercial port along the profitable 'salt road' is today a popular stop for pleasure boats along the Channel-Atlantic waterway. Take time to stroll along the steep, narrow streets of the old town dominating the River Vilaine and centred round the place Bouffay. The modern suspension bridge offers lovely views of the meandering river.

43km southeast of Vannes on the N165.

Rochefort-en-Terre

This small village, set on a promontory, is a gem of domestic architecture, solid 16th- and 17th-century granite houses brightened by a profusion of red geraniums everywhere: around the well, in stone troughs along the streets, and pouring over balconies. Notice the elegant gabled façade of the church, which contains a late Gothic rood screen. All that is left of the château is the gatehouse and some outbuildings restored by a recent American owner, the painter Alfred Klots, who turned them into a museum of *objets d'art* and furniture.

Château tel: 02 97 43 35 05.
Open: Jul & Aug 10am–7pm; Jun & Sep 2–7pm.

Rochefort-en-Terre is 31km east of Vannes on the N166, D775, & D777.

St-Nazaire

Old St-Nazaire was all but obliterated by Allied bombing. The main interest for visitors is the harbour – more precisely, the terrace offering panoramic views of the harbour and the Loire estuary. The nearby museum, devoted to the history of shipbuilding, includes a tour of the submarine *Espadon*, the first French vessel to sail beneath the polar ice cap.

53km west of Nantes on the N165 and N171. The Espadon *is on ave St-Hubert. Tel: 08 10 88 84 44.*
Open: 9.30am–12.30pm & 1.30–7pm.

Vannes

See pp136–7.

Artist's dream: the grey stone of Rochefort-en-Terre framed with an abundance of floral colour

Walk: Old Nantes

This walk explores the historic heart of the ancient capital of Brittany. Here, during the 15th century, the last Dukes built two impressive monuments – the magnificent castle and the cathedral – as a symbol of their power. Five centuries later, these are still the city's most imposing landmarks.

Allow 2 hours, excluding a visit to the castle.

Start from the place St-Pierre.

1 Cathédrale St-Pierre

The finely carved portals, in true Flamboyant style, contrast with the stocky outline of the towers. Notice the statue of St Peter in the middle of the central portal. Inside, the use of white stone comes as a welcome surprise in a region where granite is common. The tall nave is in harmony with the vertical lines of the simple pillars, which merge directly into the elegant vaulting. In the south transept is the funeral monument of François II and his wife, Marguerite de Foix, a Renaissance masterpiece

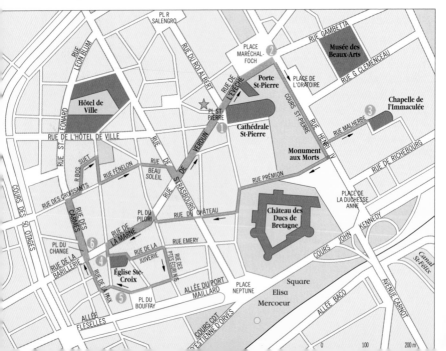

commissioned by their daughter, the Duchess Anne, and carved by Michel Colombe between 1502 and 1507.

Adjacent to the south side of the cathedral is the 15th-century chapterhouse known as La Psalette.
Proceed along the north side of the cathedral.

2 Place Maréchal-Foch

Notice on your right the Porte St-Pierre, a handsome gatehouse that formed part of the town's fortifications. Beyond is the vast place Maréchal-Foch surrounded by elegant 18th-century residences and with good views of the cathedral.
Turn right into the rue Henri IV, then take the second street on the left.

3 Chapelle de l'Immaculée

In spite of its classical façade, this chapel was built in the 15th century by the last Duke of Brittany, François II. It stands at the centre of a picturesque old district.

Return to the rue Henri IV, cross over and walk past the castle along rue Prémion, turning left then right into rue du Château, which has two beautiful residences at Nos 3 and 14. Walk across the place du Pilori into the rue de la Marne and turn left.

4 Église Ste-Croix

The classical façade of the 17th-century church looks out of place in this district, with its narrow streets and disparate houses surviving from the Middle Ages. Look up at the belfry topped with angels sounding trumpets. Walk down the rue de la Juiverie, a reminder that this was the medieval Jewish quarter, and explore

Nantes' present Gothic cathedral was begun in the 15th century but completed much later

the adjacent streets where the ancient shops and guilds have given way to restaurants, crêperies, and snack bars. The lovely old corbelled houses here are faced with slate.
Walk right round to the place du Bouffay.

5 Place du Bouffay

This was medieval Nantes' main square, where a market was held, money was minted, and justice was rendered. During the Revolution, a guillotine was the gruesome centrepiece!
Cross the square, follow the short rue du Bouffay and turn right into the rue de la Paix. Cross the rue de la Marne.

6 The Change Quarter

Just beyond the rue de la Marne lies the tiny place du Change. One of the best-preserved 15th-century houses is called the Maison des Apothicaires (Apothecaries' House). On the left is the pedestrianised rue des Halles. Continue straight on along the rue des Carmes, then turn right to explore the rue Bossuet, where No. 5 is particularly interesting.
Walk right round, then turn left to return to the place St-Pierre.

Walk: Vannes Old Town

Built on a hillside overlooking the Golfe du Morbihan, Vannes's historic centre complements the narrow harbour, the business and administrative area, and the large park adjoining the tiny River Marle below the fortifications. Two major events in this city shaped Brittany's destiny. In the 9th century Vannes became Brittany's first capital when the warrior chieftain Nominoë united the region's tribes to form a powerful independent state. In 1532 the Act of Union with France, which allowed the new province to retain some of its former independence, was signed in Vannes. This walk takes you *intra muros* (within the walls). *Allow 2 hours.*

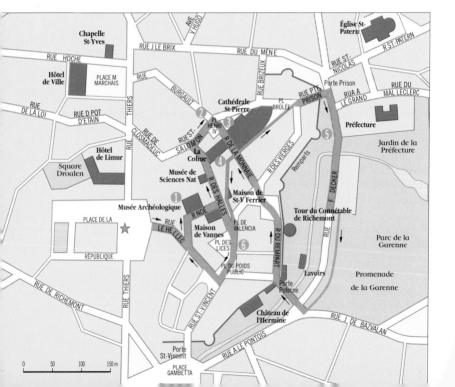

Start from the place de la République.
Walk along the rue Le Hellec and turn left.

1 Musée Archéologique

Housed in a large 15th-century
residence known as the Château
Gaillard, where the Breton Parliament
met in the 15th and 16th centuries, the
museum contains a fine collection of
prehistoric objects including some
jewels, and a separate collection of arms
and various medieval objects. At the
corner of the rue Noé and rue Rogue,
look for the two happy faces of 'Vannes
and His Wife', who have been watching
passers-by since the 15th century.
Turn left into the rue des Halles, half
taken up by tables and chairs outside
small restaurants. Turn right.

2 Place Henri IV

This former 'goat's hill' (the name
probably derives from pagan rites held
here in ancient times) is a charming
square surrounded by timber-framed
houses dating from the 15th to the 17th
centuries. At the corners, the overhangs
are so close that the roofs almost touch.

3 Cathédrale St-Pierre

The cathedral dates mainly from the
15th century. The round chapel on the
north side is one of the rare examples of
Italian Renaissance style in Brittany; it
contains the grave of St Vincent Ferrier,
a Spanish monk who preached and died
in Vannes and was later canonised.

4 La Cohue

The old covered market going back to
the 13th century stands opposite the
cathedral. Shopkeepers' stalls used to
occupy the ground floor, while the old
Court of Justice was housed on the first
floor. Today, it is the home of the town's
museums, containing a fine collection of
paintings and illustrating local history.
Walk along the south side of the cathedral
to the Porte Prison.

5 The Town Walls

The Porte Prison is one of the original
gates leading out of the old town. From
the rue Francis Decker the walls can be
seen rising behind brightly patterned
flower gardens. The view is even better
from the park known as the promenade
de la Garenne. Notice the ancient wash-
house beside the stream.
Re-enter the old town through the Porte
Poterne; turn right into the rue du Rem-
part, then along the rue de la Monnaie,
and left down the rue des Orfèvres to the
place de Valencia; St Vincent Ferrier died
in No. 17 in 1419. Turn left.

6 Place des Lices

This large square gets its name from the
games and tournaments that were held
there in 1532 to celebrate the Act of
Union with France.
Cross the square and turn right. On
Wednesday and Saturday, a fruit and
vegetable market is held on the place du
Poids Public, lined with 17th- and 18th-
century houses. Continue straight on to
return to the place de la République.

La Cohue Museums 9 and 15 place St-
Pierre. *Tel: 02 97 47 35 86.* Open: 10am–
6pm in summer. Admission charge.
Musée Archéologique 2 rue Noé.
Tel: 02 97 42 59 80. Open: Jun–Sep
10am–6pm. Admission charge.

Tour: Castles of Southern Brittany

This 132-km tour focuses on four very different castles and two ancient towns. It offers a look at the lifestyle of the Dukes of Brittany and their powerful vassals, but also of the craftsmen and merchants who made up the backbone of Breton society from the 14th century onwards.

Allow a full day.

Start from Vannes, former residence of the Dukes of Brittany. Drive east on the D779 for about 6km and turn south towards the Presqu'île de Rhuys.

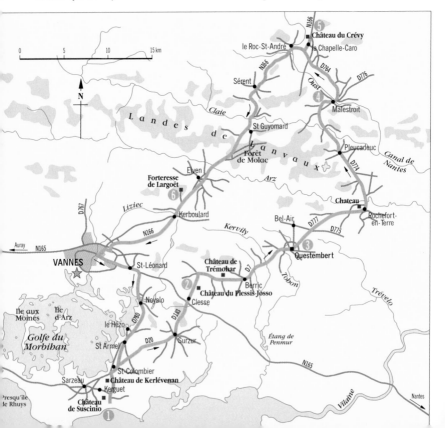

1 Château de Suscinio

This imposing and austere feudal castle was once the favourite summer residence and hunting lodge of the Dukes of Brittany. Built at the beginning of the 13th century, it was remodelled and extended by several dukes, seized and dismantled by du Guesclin, confiscated by the King of France, and damaged during the Revolution. Its high walls and impressive towers still stand facing the open sea, which used to fill the moat at every tide. Round the courtyard, the living quarters have lost their roofs and flooring. The restored gatehouse contains a historical museum with a rare collection of ceramic tiles from the 13th and 14th centuries. From the top of the largest tower there are fine views.
Return to the main road and bear right on the D20, then left at Surzur on the D183.

2 Château du Plessis-Josso

This is a typical Breton manor house, built in the 14th century by a member of the Duke of Brittany's household and extended later. It shows the evolution of a noble family's way of life from the austere feudal period to the more sociable 17th century.
Drive on and turn right on the D7.

3 Questembert

The old city nestles round the fine 16th-century *halles* (covered market), a reminder of the cloth trade that brought prosperity to Questembert. Notice the fine granite houses, including the Hôtel de Belmont, now the tourist office. Down the rue St-Michel, you can see carved on a turret a couple of figures nicknamed *Questembert et sa femme*

(Questembert and his wife).
At Rochefort-en-Terre (see p133), turn left on the D774.

4 Malestroit

It was here that a truce was signed between the French and English kings during the Hundred Years' War. The Chapelle de la Madeleine, where it took place, is now in ruins. Around the church are half-timbered houses from the 15th to 17th centuries.
Drive north on the D764.

5 Château du Crévy

Built in the 14th century but remodelled several times, this pleasant manor now houses a *musée du costume* with a dazzling collection of costumes from the 18th century to the present day.
Drive southwest on the N166.

6 Forteresse de Largoët

These splendid ruins consist of the gatehouse and one of the tallest keeps in France. In summer it is the romantic setting for a *Son et Lumière* show based on the story of Tristan and Isolde.
Return to Vannes on the N166.

Château de Suscinio
Tel: 02 97 41 91 91. Open: all year round at 10am. Closing times vary (check on phone). Admission charge.
Château du Plessis-Josso
Tel: 02 97 43 16 16. Open: Jul & Aug 2–7pm; out of season ring for information.
Château du Crévy
Tel: 02 97 74 91 95. Open: Jul & Aug 10am–6pm; Apr–Oct, Wed & weekends 2–6pm. Admission charge.
Forteresse de Largoët
Tel: 02 97 53 35 96. Open: Feb–Nov 10.30am–6.30pm.

Getting Away From It All

Everyone dreams of getting away from it all at one time or another, and there are many different ways to realise that dream. But most of us agree on certain essential ingredients: peace and quiet – even solitude – freedom, space, and, most important of all, unspoilt nature. Brittany has more than its fair share of all these, if you know where to look, and the variety of its natural environment means there's something to suit every taste.

Razorbills are among the migrating species that can be seen from March to July on Ile Grande

In Brittany you can glide along a canal or sail on foamy waves; you can lose yourself in birdwatching, listen for Merlin's harp, or look for elves under huge boulders in the ancient forests of Celtic legend; you can feel at peace with the world in the mellow English-style park of a great castle; or you can walk back in time along the cobbled streets of Brittany's many medieval towns.

BIRD RESERVES AND ISLAND TRIPS

The coastline of Brittany and its offshore islands provide sanctuaries for a variety of seabirds, both resident and migrating (*see pp144–5*). The places listed below are just a sampling of the region's bird reserves.

Côtes d'Armor

Les Sept Iles This group of islands has the only colony of gannets in France (9,000 pairs), as well as puffins, guillemots, and cormorants. Boat trips from Perros-Guirec, Trégastel, and Port-Blanc (*tel: 02 96 91 10 00*).

Just a few kilometres south, in Pleumeur Bodou, an information centre about the Sept Iles has a direct live video link enabling amateurs to watch the birds closely (*tel: 02 96 91 91 40*).

Finistère

Archipelago des Glénan The island of St-Nicolas is an important nesting ground that also boasts the *narcisse des Glénan*, a unique species of narcissus. Boat trips from Bénodet, Concarneau, Loctudy: Vedettes de l'Odet, Bénodet (*tel: 02 98 57 00 58*).

Goulien Cap Sizun The best months to observe puffins, cormorants and guillemots are May, June, and July. Open: 10am–noon and 2–6pm (*tel: 02 98 70 13 53*).

Molène This archipelago is mostly known for its grey seals and dolphins. Boat trips from Le Conquet: Compagnie Penn ar Bed (*tel: 02 98 80 80 80*).

Morbihan

Ile de Groix The reserve is open from June to September (*tel: 02 97 86 55 97*). Information about boat trips from Compagnie Morbihannaise de Navi-ation, Lorient (*tel: 08 20 05 60 00*).

Belle-Ile At Koh-Castell on the Côte Sauvage is one of Brittany's best colonies of seabirds. Open: July and August daily (except Monday). Direct link Lorient-Sauzon (*tel: 02 97 21 03 97*).

Séné Look for signposts from the village. Open: July and August 10am–1pm and 2–6pm. Information from tourist office in Vannes (*tel: 02 97 47 24 34*).

FORESTS

Cool green forests are among the most memorable features of inland Brittany, with their rocks, ravines and quiet streams.

Carnoët

Situated on the west bank of the River Laïta, between Quimperlé and le Pouldu, this lush forest offers a network of paths for walking and riding. The Rocher Royal, near Toulfoën, commands good views of the river and the ruins of Carnoët Castle, which legend claims was the home of the local Bluebeard.

Fougères

Covering 1,600 hectares north of Fougères, this woodland is part of the ancient Forest of Scissy, strongly associated with the Druids; among the tall beech trees can be found several megaliths and Gallic ruins. There are marked footpaths and an outdoor leisure centre. Information about guided tours from tourist office in Fougères (*tel: 02 99 94 12 20*).

Gâvre

This forest of 4,500 hectares north of Blain is ideal for walking, cycling, and horse riding. Hunts sometimes take place, so you might spot one in progress.

Pointe-du-Raz looks out on the low-lying Ile de Sein; its islanders live exclusively by fishing

Huelgoat

Huelgoat Forest is scattered with huge boulders, sometimes piled in precarious-looking arrangements over which tumbles an unruly stream. It makes a delightful place to stroll and meditate in. Paths follow the canal and the Rivière d'Argent (Silver River), which gets its name from the former silver mines, and lead to delightful spots with poetic names like Trou du Diable (Devil's Hole), Roche Tremblante (Trembling Rock), or Camp d'Artus, an overgrown Gallo-Roman camp where, according to legend, a fabulous treasure discovered by King Arthur is buried.

Paimpont

This is the legendary Forest of Brocéliande, one of the most mysterious Breton settings of the famous tales of King Arthur and the Knights of the Round Table.

Discover the Fontaine de Barenton, where Merlin met the enchantress Viviane; the Château de Comper, where Viviane brought up Lancelot; Merlin's grave; and the Val Sans Retour and its lake, called the Miroir des Fées (Fairies' Mirror), where Morgan the enchantress kept unfaithful lovers prisoner.
Information from Pays d'Accueil touristique de Brocéliande. Tel: 02 99 06 86 07.

FRENCH GARDENS AND ENGLISH-STYLE PARKS

Whether you prefer the symmetry and artistic composition of French gardens or the soothing, gently curving harmony of English-style parks, Brittany's castles can offer you both.

Bois Cornillé

This large park combines both French and English styles with a pond, a lake, an arbour, and extensive woods.
*Val d'Izé, Ille-et-Vilaine.
Open: 7 Jul–8 Sep 10am–12.30pm & 2.30–7pm. Admission charge.*

Caradeuc

This is Brittany's biggest park, with numerous statues, monuments, and ornamental ponds among the flower beds and along the paths.
Bécherel, Ille-et-Vilaine. Tel: 02 99 66 77 76. Open: Jul–Aug noon–6pm, Sep–Oct 2–6pm. Admission charge.

Kerguéhennec

With its woods, lawns, and lakes the park provides a sympathetic setting for an exhibition of sculptures by internationally famous artists.
Bignan, Morbihan. Tel: 02 97 60 44 44. Open: Apr–Oct 10am–6pm. Closed: Mon. Admission charge.

Rosanbo

The park was beautifully redesigned in the 19th century according to plans by Le Nôtre. Note the beautiful arbours on either side of the terraces.
Lanvellec, Côtes d'Armor. Open: Apr–Jun 2–5pm, Jul & Aug 11am–6pm. Admission charge.

Trévarez

Situated at the heart of the Montagnes Noires, the setting seems out of a fairy tale, with a pink castle and a profusion of rhododendrons, camellias, azaleas, and hydrangeas – truly magical when in bloom.

St-Goazec, Finistère. Tel: 02 98 26 82 79.
Open: Apr–Sep 1–6pm, Jul & Aug
11am–6.30pm. Admission charge.

PARC NATUREL RÉGIONAL D'ARMORIQUE

Sweeping right across Finistère from the Montagnes d'Arrée through the Crozon Peninsula to the islands of Sein and Ouessant, this conservation area encompasses 172,000 hectares. Its purpose is threefold: to protect a unique environment, to allow the scientific study of that environment, and to serve as an open-air museum of nature, with various places of interest.

The Ménez-Meur estate in the Montagnes d'Arrée houses the park's information centre (Hanvec, *tel: 98 68 81 71*), a game reserve, and the Breton Horse Museum (open: June to September 10am–7pm). Also in the Monts d'Arrée is the ancient village of Moulins de Kerouat, built round a waterfall, complete with water mills and a tannery.

There are the Rural School Museum (Trégarvan, off the D60 along the Aulne estuary), the Museum of Game and Hunting (Scrignac, on the D42 north of Huelgoat), many fascinating places like the Yeun Elez (a marshland area rich in wildlife) north of Réservoir de St-Michel, and the valley of the Elorn (one of the finest salmon rivers in France), as well as Roc Trévezel (accessible from the D758), at 384m the highest peak of the Montagnes d'Arrée.

Huelgoat Forest, with its mossy rocks and cool streams, is truly fit for fairies and legends

Wildlife

The shrill cry of seabirds is a familiar sound along the coast of Brittany, and in some places they are even heard over the deafening noise of crashing waves. All year, in all weathers, they circle and soar in their thousands, an essential part of the seascape. The cliffsides where the birds nest and settle at night seem absurdly overcrowded, but the different species, whether resident or migrating, seem to have reached an amicable arrangement.

Gannets have been the focus of attention in the last few years because the island of Rouzic in the Sept-Iles archipelago is their only nesting ground in France. Video cameras have been set up on the cliff wall so that these birds, who are very shy, can be watched from the ornithological station on Ile Grande. The gannets leave in October, but shags and black-backed gulls, who are their close neighbours, stay behind.

Water birds, on the other hand, prefer another kind of habitat such as the marshy areas of the Brière and the Golfe du Morbihan, the latter having the largest concentration of birds along the whole length of the north and west coasts of France. Brent geese travel all the way from Lapland and Siberia to spend the winter in the Gulf, in company with all sorts of wild ducks. There they cohabit with waders such as oystercatchers and ringed plovers.

In springtime, an extraordinary aerial ballet – of which puffins are undoubtedly the stars – takes place in the sky over Brittany, when the winter tenants depart for their summer homes in northern countries, temporarily leaving their lodgings to those who arrive from warmer climates.

Among the many inhabitants of the islands of Molène and the Sept-Iles can be counted a small number of grey seals, quite endearing with their long moustaches and disarming look, who can be seen sunbathing on the rocks.

Birds of all kinds, from puffins to terns, find a hospitable habitat and a wealth of food in the coastal and inland regions of Brittany; facing page: a grey seal pup takes a nap in the sun

PARC NATUREL RÉGIONAL DE BRIÈRE

This extensive marshland, situated a few kilometres inland from la Baule, is criss-crossed by shallow canals and shaded by tall reeds. Most of its 22,000 hectares has belonged to the 21 local communities since the 15th century. The inhabitants lived by farming, hunting, and fishing, using peat for fuel and reeds for roofing.

Today, most of the residents work in the neighbouring towns and the marsh is gaining ground. The long flat boats are still the only means of transport to get across; organised boat trips are available. (Information from Office de Tourisme de Brière, La Chapelle des Marais, *tel: 02 40 66 85 01*).

At Rozé, which was the marsh's main port, you can visit the Maison de l'Eclusier (Lock-keeper's House), which explains the geology, history, fauna, and flora of the Brière. Nearby, in the Parc Animalier (Animal Reserve), a footpath leads you to the heart of the marsh, where you can observe the behaviour of birds and other animal (*tel: 02 40 91 17 80;* guided tours in July and August, 9.30am, 2.30pm, and 4.30pm; admission charge).

Nearby on the Ile de Fédrun, the Maison de la Marée shows displays of old-time wedding customs (admission charge).

On the western edge of the marsh, Kerhinet is a traditional village with charming thatched cottages authentically restored. The Chaumière des Saveurs et de l'Artisanal displays a range of local handicrafts (*tel: 02 40 61 95 24*).

A boat tour of the Brière Regional Nature Park reveals the fascinating life of the marshland

Alternatively, tour Brière by horse and cart

PEACEFUL INLAND TOWNS
Experience the unhurried pace of life in the past by visiting centuries-old towns that have kept their character. All have special treasures for you to discover.

Bécherel
This feudal town prospered from the manufacture of linen yarn. Stately merchants' houses, particularly round the marketplace, certainly testify to its thriving past. Notice their turrets and fine gables. The Château de Caradeuc is nearby (see p142).
31km northwest of Rennes.

Châtelaudren
Once the commercial centre of the coastal strip between Paimpol and St-Brieuc, Châtelaudren used to hold lively fairs and markets. This explains the splendour of the church of Notre-Dame-du-Tertre, built in the 14th century, whose vaulting is covered with 132 painted panels of rare quality and refinement.
17km west of St-Brieuc.

Guerlesquin
From its days as an important market town, Guerlesquin has retained an unusually large central square. In addition to a lively weekly market, the town held 19 annual fairs, specialising in wine, linen and horses. The imposing *présidial* (a former prison) was a status symbol and now forms a pleasing group with the market and the church.
23km southeast of Morlaix.

Jugon-les-Lacs
A quaint charm pervades this sleepy little town built on the edge of a large lake and surrounded by woodland. The place du Martray and the Maison Sevoy, a splendid 17th-century residence, are the only reminders of the town's former importance, which worried Richelieu so much that he had the fortress razed to the ground in 1616.
21km west of Dinan.

Lizio
Lizio is now only a modest village but, from its past as a centre of the cloth trade, it has preserved a handsome ensemble of 17th- and 18th-century domestic architecture. Today, it hosts Brittany's largest Fête des Artisans d'Art (Crafts Festival) in August.
32km northeast of Vannes.

Malestroit
See p139.

Moncontour
See p77.

Questembert
See p139.

Old tidal mill near St Suliac, a forerunner of the Rance Tidal Power scheme near Dinard

RIVERS AND CANALS

After centuries of intense commercial activity, Brittany's navigable rivers and canals, totalling 600km, are now solely used for pleasure cruising, and the old towpaths look strangely deserted.

An increasing number of holidaymakers are rediscovering the pleasures of river travel, and cruising at 6 to 10km per hour has become for many a new philosophy of life, a pleasant way to counter that growing sense of anxiety that would otherwise climax with a plea to 'stop the world, I want to get off'!

Two main waterways cross Brittany from north to south and from east to west: the Channel-Atlantic Link and the Nantes-Brest Canal. The Channel-Atlantic Link between St-Malo and the Arzal Dam in the Vilaine estuary is 239km long, the most picturesque sections being the Rance estuary, Hédé and its 11 successive locks, and the valley of the Vilaine between Rennes and Redon. Main towns on the way are Dinan, Rennes, Redon, and La Roche-Bernard.

The 360-km long Nantes-Brest Canal has been split into two separate sections ever since the building of the Guerlédan Dam. The east section runs from Nantes to Pontivy, then down the Blavet to Lorient going through Redon, Malestroit and Josselin. The most attractive part lies between Redon and Pontivy, along the Oust valley. The west section links Carhaix-Plouguer to Brest via the canalised River Aulne, which meanders through Châteaulin.

For detailed information contact the Comité des Canaux Bretons, Office du Tourisme, place du Parlement, 35600 Redon (tel: 02 99 71 06 04). Tourisme Fluvial en Bretagne, a brochure available in tourist offices gives charges and addresses of boat-hire companies.

WATER MILLS AND OTHER MILLS

The Morbihan département contains a wealth of old water mills, tidal mills, and windmills, along the coast and inland. Their discovery through well-planned itineraries can be a delightful way to relax by going back to a time when nature set the pace. A brochure is available from tourist offices.

Sailing and fishing boats at Cap Sizun

Shopping

Brittany is no longer the remote economic entity it used to be. As one of the main regions of France it has a well-balanced economy, thriving commercial activities and a wide range of shops, from vast hypermarkets to small boutiques.

Floor-to-ceiling stock in the village of Locronan

Practical Information

Shops stay open late in France, and Brittany is no exception. In towns they are usually open until 7pm, food shops until 8pm or even later, although they may close on Monday morning or all day Monday (although this is unlikely during the high season).

Department stores are, of course, more rigid about their opening hours, which are usually 9–9.30am to 6.30–7pm. In tourist areas, souvenir and clothes shops may stay open late in the evening.

As shops accept most credit cards, there is no need to carry a lot of cash unless you're heading for a market or fair. Prices are more or less in line with those of other French regions.

Hypermarkets

Hypermarkets first appeared in France about 30 years ago, and they've been growing in number and in size ever since, gradually absorbing a huge share of the market. Located on the outskirts of most towns, they provide a Saturday outing for many families. The usually excellent cafeterias have a special children's menu, and the fare is much better than the British equivalent or fast-food restaurants (and just as cheap), including salads, fresh fruit, pastries and sundaes.

Among the most obvious advantages of hypermarkets are late closing times, low prices, and the tremendous choice of goods available, from food and kitchen/dining items to hi-fi, clothes, garden furniture, tools, paint, and even car tyres – not forgetting cheap petrol outside. There are often over 50 cash desks, and one or two are usually reserved for customers with fewer than 10 articles so they can avoid huge queues.

Some of these jumbo stores are surrounded with independent boutiques selling shoes, clothes, china and sportswear as well as services like hairdressing, dry-cleaning, and shoe repair. Altogether they form a *centre commercial* that may have one or two other restaurants besides the hypermarket's cafeteria. France has several chains of hyper-markets, though not all of them are represented in Brittany. The most common names you will see written in huge letters across the countryside in Brittany are Carrefour, Intermarché, Auchan and Leclerc – one of the best for quality and price, founded by Edouard Leclerc, a native of Landerneau in Finistère.

Supermarkets

Supermarché is the term used for a much smaller general store, where little other than food is sold. These shops have existed longer than hypermarkets and are well integrated in smaller towns, usually run by local people but belonging to a regional or national chain. Prices are higher than in hypermarkets, but service – by a new generation of village grocers – is more personal.

Shopping in Main Towns

The most fashionable shopping centres are in Rennes, Nantes, and Quimper, where elegant boutiques are further elevated by historic surroundings. Most sell luxury goods, but don't be surprised if names like Benetton, Lacoste, and Hermès sound vaguely familiar. Fashion boutiques, with zappy names like Energie in Concarneau and Cassidy, are also found in Rennes and Quimper.

The small shops and galleries that abound in Locronan sell specialities from soap to hand-carved saints

Markets

Colourful, sociable, and lively, markets have a sense of occasion that everyone enjoys. Market squares everywhere suddenly take on a new dimension on market day, becoming the ideal place to dawdle and waste time (purposefully!), to listen, observe, to laugh, and to marvel at life's simplicity.

Markets take place once or twice a week in towns and villages in Brittany, the particular day of the week varying from one place to the next to allow people a chance to attend them all, if they so wish!

Local farmers and itinerant sellers set up stalls of all kinds on the main square, and often in adjacent streets as well. The sophisticated ones announce themselves with bright canopies, but most of the time goods are just laid out in a jumble exposed to the morning sun.

Vegetables of all sorts rub shoulders with beautiful flowers, T-shirts, and trinkets, cutlery, and gadgets, live chickens and dead ones. Special display vans offer appetising *charcuterie*,

including chipolatas sold by the metre, and tantalising cheeses, with unfamiliar names, that look irresistible.

The background noise of voices and laughter swells to its loudest around 11.30am, then decreases as housewives tear themselves away to return home to cook the inescapable midday meal. The stallkeepers then start packing up and by 1pm the square is deserted.

Main Weekly Markets
Some of these last all day.

CÔTES D'ARMOR
Châtelaudren Monday morning
Dinan Thursday morning
Guingamp Friday morning and Saturday all day
Jugon-les-Lacs Friday morning
Lannion Thursday morning and afternoon
Moncontour Monday morning
Pontrieux Monday
Quintin Tuesday
St-Brieuc Wednesday and Saturday morning
Tréguier Wednesday morning.

FINISTÈRE
Audierne Saturday morning
Bénodet Monday morning
Brest Friday; every morning in the Halles St-Louis and St-Martin
Carhaix Saturday and Wednesday morning for local produce
Châteaulin Thursday
Concarneau Monday and Friday morning
Daoulas Sunday morning
Douarnenez Monday and Saturday morning

Embroidered *sabots* for sale in Batz-sur-Mer

Fouesnant Friday.
Guerlesquin Monday morning
Le Guilvinec Tuesday morning
Landerneau Tuesday and Friday
  morning, Saturday all day
Landivisiau Wednesday
Loctudy Tuesday morning
Morlaix Saturday
Pont-Aven Tuesday morning
Pont l'Abbé Thursday
Quimper Everyday, Halle Centrale
Quimperlé Friday
Roscoff Wednesday morning
St-Pol-de-Léon Tuesday.

ILLE-ET-VILAINE

Bécherel Saturday morning
Cancale Sunday morning
Châteaugiron Thursday morning
Combourg Monday morning
Dinard Saturday morning
Dol-de-Bretagne Saturday morning
Fougères Saturday morning
Redon Monday, Friday and Saturday
Rennes Saturday morning
St-Malo Tuesday, Friday and Saturday
Vitré Monday morning; local produce
  on Saturday morning.

LOIRE-ATLANTIQUE

Châteaubriant Wednesday morning
Guérande Wednesday and Saturday
  morning
Le Croisic Tuesday, Thursday and
  Saturday morning under the covered
  market
Nantes every morning except Monday;
  Wednesday, Saturday and Sunday
  all day.

MORBIHAN

Auray Monday, Friday, and Sunday

Brittany's renowned fruit and vegetables can be seen in all their glory in the market

  morning (one of the most important
  in Brittany)
Hennebont Thursday morning
Josselin Saturday morning
La Roche-Bernard Thursday morning
Malestroit Thursday morning
Pontivy Monday morning and
  afternoon
La Trinité-sur-Mer Tuesday and Friday
Vannes Wednesday, Saturday morning.

Specialised Markets

Bécherel (Ille-et-Vilaine): *marché aux
  livres* (books) on the first Sunday of
  the month
Dinan (Côtes d'Armor): *marché aux
  puces* (bric-à-brac) every Wednesday
  in July and August, place St-Sauveur
Fougères (Ille-et-Vilaine): *marché de
  l'aumaillerie* (cattle) every Friday
  morning from 5am
Lizio (Morbihan): Fête des Artisans
  d'Art (handicrafts) on the second
  Sunday in August.

Breton Specialities

Apart from the usual souvenirs, shops in every corner of Brittany offer a wealth of local products – a pleasure to look at, if not to take back home.

Antiques
Les Aristos Broc's
Rue de Closmadeuc, Vannes.
Tel: 02 97 54 30 57.
Jacques Morin
32 rue St-Guillaume, St-Brieuc.
Tel: 02 96 61 81 95.
Desury
16 rue du Gouët, St-Brieuc.
Tel: 02 96 61 46 74.
Hénaux
25 rue St-Guillaume, St-Brieuc.
Tel: 02 96 33 07 90.
Olivier Delouche
2 place Gasnier-Dupare, St-Malo.
Tel: 02 99 40 01 02.

Boats
Le Lionnais Marine
Boats, engines, and gear.
Port de Paimpol.
Tel: 02 96 20 85 18.

Breton Products
Comptoir des Produits Bretons
Traditional objects.
3 Quai de Cornouaille, Landerneau.
Tel: 02 98 21 35 93.
Biscuterie La Trinitaine
Traditional Breton biscuits and food.
Saint Philibert, La Trinité-sur-Mer.
Le Comptoir alte
Traditional Breton products.
8 rue Saint-Vincent, Vannes.
Tel: 02 97 01 05 04.

Ceramics and Pottery
Art de Cornouaille
A wide choice of HB Henriot ceramics.
12 Place St-Corentin, Quimper.
Tel: 02 98 95 39 24.
Faïenceries de Quimper
Ceramics.
9 Rue Haute, Quimper.
Tel: 02 98 90 09 36.
Gwen et Dodik
Painted ceramics.
4 rue Chateaubriand, St-Malo. Tel: 02 99 56 68 82.
Fanch Griffon
Earthenware, glass, and crystal.
4 rue Dugay-Trouin, Douarnenez.
Tel: 02 98 92 18 17.
Faïence HB Henriot
Ceramics.
Place Bérardier, Locmaria, Quimper.
Tel: 02 98 52 22 52.
Monique Léon
Pottery workshop.
9 rue Réveillère, Roscoff.
Tel: 02 98 69 73 13.

FAÏENCE DE QUIMPER

Quimper's first ceramic workshop was founded more than 300 years ago, but today, Quimper ceramics are a mixture of styles from other parts of France, in particular, Moustiers in Provence, Nevers in central France, and Rouen in Normandy.

Later, in the 19th century, an artist decided to decorate Quimper ceramics with typical Breton scenes. In 1968, two of the original manufacturers merged to become HB Henriot, today the most famous *faïencerie*. Although it was taken over by an American firm in 1984, local artists continue to decorate and sign each piece.

Pierette et J Paul Soulet
Pottery workshop.
6 rue Carnot, Vannes.
Tel: 02 97 47 56 08.

Food
See pp168–9.

Lace
Mercerie Lagadic
Lace, tablecloths, and
doilies.
30 rue René-Madec,
Quimper.
Tel: 02 98 95 61 22.

Paper
Moulin de Pen-Mur
Traditional paper
manufacture.
Muzillac, Morbihan.
Tel: 97 41 43 79.

**Sailing Clothes and
Gear**
Armor Lux
Breton striped clothing.
60 bis rue Guy Autret,
Quimper.
Tel: 02 98 90 05 29.
Le Glazik
Traditional overcoats.
9 rue du 19 Mars 1962,
Quimper.
Tel: 02 98 52 29 28.
Héoligou
Clothes, sportswear,
hand-knitted sweaters.
16 rue du Parc, Quimper.
Tel: 02 98 95 13 29.
Kristel
Hand-knitted sweaters.
7 rue des Boucheries,
Quimper.

Tel: 02 98 95 01 92.
Richard Marine
Ship's chandler.
3 rue du Glorioux,
St-Malo.
Tel: 02 99 81 63 81.

**Stained Glass and
Crafts**
Christine Cocar
63 rue Maréchal-Foch,
St-Brieuc.
Tel: 02 96 60 45 72.
Verrerie de Bréhat
La Citadelle, Bréhat.
Tel: 02 96 20 09 09.

There are several fine
craft shops in the ancient
cities of Locronan and
Rochefort-en-Terre.

Painted pottery makes a pretty, useful memento

Entertainment

Traditions are so much a part of daily life in Brittany that they form the basis of the region's rich and varied choice of entertainment. Visitors appreciate being able to share in the spontaneous enjoyment of a people who still celebrate life as their ancestors did.

Traditional instruments and dances are complemented by regional costumes

Music and Dance

Inseparable as they are, music and dance make up the main, most delightful ingredient of traditional festivals. Breton music goes back to Celtic times, and some of the instruments, such as the Celtic harp, have remained unchanged.

Among all the others, the *biniou* is the best known outside Brittany; a bagpipe with one or three drones, it has a somewhat shrill tone. A *biniou* is often accompanied by a *bombarde*, a kind of oboe, this duo being the most commonly found at dance sessions. The *treujenn gaol*, on the other hand, is a type of clarinet that became popular during the 19th century and is still very much appreciated today. Two more instruments play an important role in Breton music, although they are by no means native: the accordion and the fiddle. Instrumentalists are called *sonneurs*.

Breton folk songs bear the influence of medieval plainsong and Gregorian chant, and are either slow and sad or very rhythmic and joyful. Singers often accompany dancers as in the *Kan ha Diskan*, a mountain dance in which two singers in turn increase the pace of the dance to the point of frenzy.

There are many kinds of dance,

multiplying into regional variations: the very rhythmic *gavotte* (also danced in other regions of France), the more fluid *bal*, and the slow *laridé*. Some of these dances are quite strenuous and require great skill, like the men-only *jabadao* and the *piler lan*. Modern Bretons get very little chance to practise their dancing nowadays, and the dancers seen at folk festivals are usually professional groups who give dazzling displays.

Sons et Lumière and Historical Shows

This kind of spectacle is designed to bring back to life the architectural heritage of a town or a castle through various audiovisual effects, sometimes assisted by actors in splendid costumes. Chosen themes centre on a well-known legend or on a specific period that marked the town's finest hour. The following are among the most interesting.

Dinan (Côtes d'Armor): 'Fête des Remparts'. Medieval feast in the streets of Dinan in September (*tel: 02 96 39 22 43*).

Elven (Morbihan): 'Tristan et Iseult'. Son et Lumière show at the ruins of Largoët fortress on Friday and Saturday in July and August (*tel: 02 97 53 52 79*).

Château de Kerjean (Finistère): 'Les Nuits de Kerjean: Fêtes et Légendes'. Historical show on Friday night throughout the summer (*tel: 02 98 69 93 69*).

Malestroit (Morbihan): 'Les Grandes Heures de Malestroit'. Historical show in July (*tel: 02 97 75 14 57*).

Moncontour (Côtes d'Armor): 'Fête Médiévale'. Medieval feast in August (*tel: 02 96 73 41 05*).

Port-Louis (Morbihan): Son et Lumière show in front of the citadel in July–August, illustrating the history of Port-Louis since 1076 (*tel: 02 97 82 52 93*).

Quimperlé (Finistère): Historical show at the end of July based on various events (*tel: 02 98 96 04 32*).

Quintin (Côtes d'Armor): 'Grande Férie du 14 Juillet'. A 14 July spectacle on the lake and at the castle (*tel: 02 96 74 01 51*).

St-Malo (Ille-et-Vilaine): 'St-Malo, République de la Mer'. Historical show in July and August in the courtyard of the castle (*tel: 02 99 56 64 48*).

Vannes (Morbihan): 'Fêtes Historiques'. Show and fireworks in the old town during the first weekend in July (*tel: 02 97 47 47 30*).

Celtic roots live on in Pont l'Abbé: during its Fête des Brodeuses

Pardons

*P*ardons are the living expression of the age-old religious convictions of the Breton people. Each one is linked to a saint whose statue is kept in the local church and proudly carried at the head of the procession on the day of the *pardon*. The name refers to the *pardon* (forgiveness) that members of the congregation beg for during the religious ceremony; but it is also customary to ask for the saint's intercession or to fulfil a vow.

The procession, following a fixed itinerary, consists of a mixed crowd:

parishioners in traditional costumes, bearing banners and singing hymns, plus visiting pilgrims, and curious onlookers who get drawn in by the general enthusiasm.

Mass is celebrated some time during the day, quite often outdoors, as in Ste-Anne-la-Palud near Douarnenez. The festivities that follow the religious ceremonies include dancing, eating and drinking, Breton games, and fairground entertainment.

Among the profusion of *pardons* that take place all over Brittany, there is a distinction between ordinary *pardons*, of local interest but well worth attending if you're around because they're less crowded, and the grand *pardons*, which attract people from all over Brittany.

Ste-Anne-d'Auray in July is one of a handful of very famous *pardons* in Brittany. Like many others, it is based upon a miracle: this one occurred in 1623 when a humble farmer was shown the place where a statue of St Anne was buried. Such is also the case of the *pardon* of Notre-Dame-du-Roncier in Josselin; this time a statue of the Virgin Mary was discovered under a bramble bush. It takes place in September.

Other important *pardons* include that of St-Yves, a mystic character of

medieval Brittany, which takes place in Tréguier in May; the grand *pardon* of Ste-Anne-la-Palud (Ste Anne is the patron saint of Brittany) in August, one of Brittany's most picturesque, which includes a night procession with torches; and the grand *pardon* of Notre-Dame-du-Folgoët in September.

Facing page: people of all ages and stations in life participate in the processions
This page: villagers of la Lorette celebrate their parish *pardon*

Cultural and Popular Events

Breton cultural life also includes artistic events, exhibitions, fairs, and the quintessentially French pastime of *boules*, as well as popular events of a more general and, in some cases, international interest. The two main events of the summer take place in Rennes and Nantes in July.

Les Tombées de la Nuit (Nightfall) in Rennes promotes all artistic forms: plays, classical music, jazz, storytelling, dance, poetry, street arts, and children's shows. *Tel: 02 99 67 11 11.*

Festival International d'Été in Nantes presents different aspects of music, singing and dancing with an emphasis on contemporary international trends. *Tel: 02 40 08 01 00.*

The following is a small selection of other events.

May

Quimper: Mai Photographie, various exhibitions of photographs by French and international artists. *Tel: 02 98 53 04 05.*

St-Malo: Ettonants Voyageurs, international book fair. *Tel: 02 23 21 06 21.*

Vitré: Mois Musical, concerts in the open and some of the town's old buildings. Also Mi-Carême des Gais Lurons, carnival-style parade. *Tel: 02 99 75 04 46.*

June

Nantes: Printemps des Arts, Baroque music, singing and dancing. *Tel: 02 40 20 03 00.*

July

Dinan: Rencontres Internationales de Harpe Celtique, concerts, exhibitions,

The casino at Dinard

and competitions. *Tel: 02 96 87 69 76.*
Douarnenez: Jazz en Baie, prestigious jazz festival. *Tel: 02 98 92 13 35.*
Le Croisic: Concerts.
Tel: 02 40 23 00 70.
Moncontour: Les Mardiverdissants (free concerts on Tuesday).
Tel: 02 96 73 49 57.
Vannes: Jazz Festival.
Tel: 02 97 47 24 34.

July–August

Morlaix: Les Arts dans la Rue, festival of street arts with music, new circus, open-air theatre, and improvised performances. *Tel: 02 98 62 14 94.*
St-Malo: La Route du Rock, most important rock festival in Brittany.
Tel: 02 99 53 50 30.
Pontivy: Festival de Musique de Pontivy, classical music featuring international artists and orchestras.
Tel: 02 97 25 04 10.
Redon: Les Nocturiales, Baroque music and Gregorian chants in the abbey.
Tel: 02 99 71 06 04.
St-Malo: Festival International de Musique Sacrée, festival of sacred music in the cathedral. *Tel: 02 99 56 05 38.*

August

Guérande: Académie Internationale de Musique de Guérande, introduction to music, masterclasses, concerts.
Tel: 02 40 24 96 71.
Quimper: Semaines Musicales, concerts in various prestigious venues.
Tel: 02 98 53 04 05.

September

Dinard: British Film Festival.
Tel: 02 99 88 19 04.

Nantes: Rendez-vous de l'Erdre, free concerts and shows on the banks of the River Erdre. *Tel: 02 51 82 37 70.*
St-Malo: Quai des bulles, strip cartoon festival. *Tel: 02 99 40 39 63.*

Night Life

Brittany also offers the sort of night life you find in other modern cities. Small towns of around 3,000 inhabitants – such as Binic, Quintin, and Roscoff – have at least one cinema and several bars with snooker and billiards facilities. Larger towns with a population around 10,000, such as Landerneau, have one or more discos and/or night clubs.

The choice grows with the size of the city; for instance, Douarnenez has two cinemas and six discotheques. The main towns are even better provided. Information is available from tourist offices. If your holiday is spent in a village, the local tourist office will give you a list of *animations* (entertainment) organised by the district, including bingo and dancing, usually held in the village hall.

Casinos

Most people associate casinos with a glamour that's not exactly part of their daily routine, so they might be tempted to try their luck while on holiday. Roulette, *boule*, and blackjack are standard offerings in casinos, and also at bars, restaurants, and discos, depending on the size of the premises.

With the exception of la Baule and Bénodet, most of Brittany's casinos are on the north coast – in St-Malo, Dinard, Sables-d'Or-les-Pins, le Val-André, St-Quay-Portrieux, and Perros-Guirec.

C h i l d r e n

With its gently invigorating climate, ideal for the very young, and its wealth of outdoor activities, Brittany is a children's paradise.

Cooling off under the sun

Beaches

The most popular seaside resorts have as many as five beaches, and always one that is just right for children: sheltered, shallow, free of dangerous currents and breakers. Among the safest beaches are at Carantec, Fouesnant, Perros-Guirec, le Val-André, St-Quay-Portrieux, and Carnac-Plage, many of them equipped with beach clubs where children can join in supervised activities and enjoy themselves while you relax.

A related favourite activity must wait until the tide goes out: looking for cockles in muddy sand, watching for scurrying creatures as feet or fingers disturb tide pools, finding unusual rocks, shells, and crab claws. All they need is a bucket and they're off on a real treasure hunt!

Water and Leisure Parks

Water seems to have unlimited appeal for children, and even inland there are many leisure parks where children can enjoy watery pursuits along with other outdoor activities. Phone for times of opening.

Les Aquatides

Every variety of aqua-fun.
Les Livaudières (Loudeac). Tel: 02 96 66 14 40. Open: holidays 10am–8pm.

Armoripark

Aqualand, skating rink, pedalos, mini-golf.

Bégard, north of Guingamp, Côtes d'Armor. Tel: 02 96 45 36 36.
Open: daily, mid-Jun–Aug 11am–7pm. Admission charge.

Bretagne Pêche Loisirs

Four fishing lakes, mini-golf, free games for children.
Bains sur Oust, near Redon, Ille-et-Vilaine. Tel: 02 99 91 78 78.
Open: May–Oct 7am–7pm. Closed: Tue. Admission charge.

Cobac Parc

Water slides, ponies, train, roundabouts.
Lanhélin near Combourg, Ille-et-Vilaine. Tel: 02 99 73 80 16. Open: Apr–mid-Sep 11am–6.30pm. Admission charge.

Zoos

Branféré

Exotic animals and birds.
Northwest of la Roche-Bernard, Morbihan. Tel: 02 97 42 94 66.
Open: May–mid-Sep 9am–7pm. Admission charge.

Domaine de la Bourbansais

Zoo and children's games.
Ille-et-Vilaine. Tel: 02 99 69 40 07.
Open: Apr–Sep 10am–7pm. Admission charge.

Zooloisirs

Mammals, birds, games.
Québriac, north of Rennes, Ille-et-Vilaine. Tel: 02 99 68 10 22. Open: mid-Mar–mid-Nov 10.30am–6.30pm. Admission charge.

Museums
Aquarium
Aquarium Marin de Trégastel
Trégastel. Tel: 02 96 23 48 58.
Open: 10am–8pm. Admission charge.
Manoir de l'Automobile
A beautifully-located museum on the
history of the automobile in Brittany.
Route de Lieuron 35550, Lohéac. Tel: 02
99 34 02 32. Open: 10am–1pm & 2–7pm.
Closed: Mon. Admission charge.
Musée de la Poupée (Doll Museum)
Josselin (see p128) & 13 rue de Toulouse,
St-Malo. Tel: 02 99 40 15 51. Open: 10am–
noon & 2–7pm. Admission charge.
Mystères de la Mer
St-Malo (see p51).
Océanopolis (European Sea Centre)
Port de Plaisance du Moulin Blanc, Brest.
Tel: 02 98 34 40 40. Open: 9.30am–6pm.
Admission charge.
Océarium
Ave de Saint-Goustan, Le Croisic. Tel: 02
40 23 02 44. Open: Jun–Aug 10am–7pm.

Planétarium
8 rue des Acadiens, Nantes. Tel: 02 40 73
99 23. Open: shows at 10.30am, 2.15pm
& 3.45pm. Closed: Sun morning
& Mon. Admission charge.
Planétarium de Bretagne
Pleumeur-Bodou, near Lannion.
Tel: 02 96 15 80 30; www.planetarium-
bretagne.fr (check for timings).

Open-air Museums
Musée du Bateau (Boat Museum)
Place de l'Enfer, Douarnenez.
Tel: 02 98 92 65 20. Open: 10am–7pm.
Admission charge.
Parc de la Préhistoire
(Prehistoric Park)
Thirty life-size scenes of man, beast, and
dinosaur are set in a wooded setting;
explanations are given in English.
Malansac, near Rochefort-en-Terre.
Tel: 02 97 43 34 17. Open: Apr–mid-Oct
10am–6pm; mid-Oct–mid-Nov
1.30–6pm. Admission charge.

Children love the sea and the sand and there's usually plenty of entertainment

Sport and Leisure

Brittany's climate is admirably suited to outdoor sports, which make up one of the major attractions of a holiday in the region. The Comités Départementaux de Tourisme, which has offices in the *départements'* administrative centres, suggests holiday formulas based on various sports (*see* Theme Holidays, *p176*). A brochure entitled *Bretagne Vacances Actives* is available from the Maison de la Bretagne in Paris or the Comité Régional du Tourisme in Rennes (*see* Tourist Information, *p189*).

A game of *boules*, that classic French pastime

WATERSPORTS

Practically every one of the many bays and estuaries along Brittany's coastline has its watersports centre. Facilities usually cover sailing, windsurfing, canoeing, water-skiing, and diving.

Swimming

In some areas bathing is not practical at low tide, so get a timetable of the tides from your hotel or local tourist office. Many beaches are equipped with lifeguard stations, and a system of flags draws your attention to possible risks. A green flag means 'Safe Bathing', an orange flag means 'Be Careful', and a red flag means 'Bathing Prohibited'.

Sailing and Windsurfing

Wind is generously supplied in Brittany, and it's almost impossible to imagine a seascape without a sail in it. Many local sailing clubs and schools are suitable for beginners and proficient amateurs alike. If you sail your own ship, the weather forecast service to call is Météo Marine, *tel: (08) 36 68 08 08.*

General information and brochures are available from:

Fédération Française de Voile
55 ave Kléber, 75116 Paris.
Tel: 01 44 05 81 00.

Ligue de Voile de Bretagne
Port de Plaisance du Moulin Blanc,
29000 Brest. Tel: 02 98 02 49 67.

Comité Départemental de Voile
Maison Départementale des Sports,
13b ave de Cucillé, 35065 Rennes Cedex.
Tel: 02 99 54 67 69.

The best sailing and watersports centre in Brittany is the **Centre Nautique dés Glénan**, 8 place Philippe Vianney, 299000 Concarneau (*tel: 02 98 97 14 84;* *www.glenans.asso.fr*). Founded in 1950, this has become one of the most famous schools in the world.

Canoeing

This sport is practised along the coast as well as inland. Numerous clubs are there, as well as enthusiasts looking for a challenge (such as bypassing locks on the Nantes-Brest Canal).

Information available from: **Ligue du Canoë-Kayak** (9 rue de Ker Vech, 56300 Pontivy; *tel: 02 97 25 23 60*).

Diving

The great variety of marine fauna and flora and the presence of archaeological sites still only partially explored make deep-sea diving all the more fascinating in Brittany. For detailed information send for the brochure *Plongée Bretagne* by writing to the **Comité Régional de Tourisme de Bretagne**, 74B rue de Paris, 35069 Rennes Cedex.

Nautical Events

Apart from great transatlantic races such as the Route du Rhum and the Québec–St-Malo, many nautical events take place during the season:
May: Transmanche en Double–Aber Vrac'h (cross-Channel race).
June: Morlaix–Plymouth–Morlaix; Mini Fastnet–Aber Vrac'h.

July: Cowes–Dinard; Tour du Finistère Voile (sailing round Finistère).
Local regattas, windsurfing, and fun board competitions also take place all along the coast every year.

Fishing

More of a hobby than a sport, fishing attracts many holidaymakers. But the need to preserve future stocks has led to certain regulations, which vary from one *département* to the next. Contact your tourist office about local restrictions.

If you want to make fishing the central theme of your holiday, you might enjoy staying in one of the Hôtels Relais St-Pierre, which provide advice, information, a place to store fishing tackle, and a fishing permit. A brochure entitled *Destination Pêche* is available from the **Comité Régional du Tourisme**, 1 rue Raoul Ponchon, 35000 Rennes (*tel: 02 99 36 15 15; www.tourismebretagne.com*).

Skimming the sea on a windsurf in Camaret

Hang-gliding rewards the brave with exhilaration

Flying and Hang-gliding

There are quite a number of *áeroclubs* (flying clubs) all over Brittany, but fewer *clubs de parapente* (hang-gliding clubs). For a list of these clubs, contact the Comité Régional du Tourisme (*see address in the* Practical Guide, *p189*) or, once in Brittany, the local tourist office.

LAND SPORTS
Golf

Once the privilege of a few, golf has become increasingly popular in France. Courses have sprouted all over the country, but in Brittany they have a special appeal because of the vast open spaces, undulating countryside, and refreshing climate. Some courses, built right on the edge of the ocean, offer views reminiscent of Scottish or Irish courses.

You can get detailed information on all golf courses in Brittany in the brochure entitled *Golfs de Bretagne* available from the Comité Régional de Tourisme de Bretagne, 1 rue Raoul Ponchon, 35000 Rennes Cedex.

Issued for a period of three, four, or six days, the Green Pass Formule Golf lets you play on any of the associated courses as many times as you wish during the period stated on the pass (for more information, contact **Formule Golf**, *www.formule-golf.com*).

Hiking

La Bretagne à pied (Brittany on Foot) is a series of itineraries with accommo-dation suggested in the brochure *Formules Randonnée*, available from the **Maison de la Bretagne** in Paris or the **Comité Régional du Tourisme** in Rennes (*see p189 for addresses*).

Brittany has a dense network of marked paths, well maintained and used all year round. *Sentiers de grande randonnée* (marked GR on maps) cross the region in all directions, while *sentiers de petite randonnée* (marked PR) are short round-trip hikes up to 25km long.

These itineraries are described in comprehensive guides sold in some bookshops, most tourist offices, and at the Maison de la Randonnée, 9 rue des Portes Mordelaises, 35000 Rennes (*tel: 02 99 31 59 44*; open 9.30am–noon and 2–7pm, closed Sunday). They also publish a free information leaflet called *Randonnée Info*. In addition, each *département* publishes its own guide, free from the Comité Départemental du Tourisme (*see p189*).

Cycling

Cycling the minor roads of inland Brittany is also one of the favourite activities of holidaymakers. For those who prefer riding mountain bikes, guides describing the network of special paths are available as for the hiking guides above. An additional useful address is: **Fédération Française de Cyclotourisme** (Ligue de Bretagne), 1 rue de Vau Louis BP12 22001 St Brieuc Cédex1 (*tel: 02 96 94 03 29*).

Riding

If you want to spend your holiday on horseback, then you need to get the brochure *Formules Cheval* which is available from the Comité Régional du Tourisme de Bretagne (*see p189*).

Alternatively, numerous riding centres throughout Brittany offer a wide choice of short and long treks for both beginners and experienced riders. Information from: **La France à Cheval**, Formules Bretagne, 203 boulevard Saint Germain 75007 Paris (*tel: 01 53 63 11 53*); and from **Poney Club de France**, 30 ave d'I'éra, Paris (*tel: 01 53 67 44 44*).

During the season, several national and international horse-jumping competitions are held in Dinard, La Trinité-sur-Mer, Rennes, Fougères, Vannes, and many other places. Two of the most famous stud farms in Brittany which you might like to visit are:

Haras de Hennebont, rue Victor Hugo, 56700 Hennebont (*tel: 02 97 36 20 27*); and Haras de Lamballe, place du Champ de Foire, 22405 Lamballe (*tel: 02 96 31 00 40*).

Tennis

Most holiday resorts, however small, have public tennis courts. Enquire from the local tourist office or the *mairie* (Town Hall).

Riding in Roc Trévezel

Food and Drink

Brittany's cuisine is reputed for its quality rather than its variety. Some people make the droll comment that Breton culinary traditions can be summed up in one word: *crêpes*. There is a grain of truth in this assumption. For a long time the choice of local produce was, broadly speaking, limited to seafood along the coast and cereals and pork inland.

Muscadet or cider along with your meal

Apparently, even the powerful Breton imagination could not overcome the situation, and the staple diet consisted of wholesome stews such as pork-and-buckwheat, *kig-ha-fars*. But things have changed for the better here as food production has diversified and the region has prospered generally.

Fish and Seafood

Fishmongers' stalls are one of the unforgettable sights of Brittany, laden with rainbow displays of fish large and small, a harvest from the sea, rivers, and mountain streams. The choice is bewildering: sole, skate, sardines, turbot, mackerel, bream, caught daily along the coast, salmon from the Aulne and Scorff rivers, trout from mountain areas, and pike from the Loire.

Shellfish is also one of the great delicacies, particularly where it's served in small harbour restaurants shortly after leaving the quayside. Lobsters, prawns, and scallops are plentiful, and Breton chefs make a point of inventing new mouth-watering ways of preparing them. Oysters bred along the coast are served *nature* (plain) with a few drops of lemon juice, either on their own or as part of a *plateau de fruits de mer*

(seafood selection), which can be a meal in itself. Cooked mussels, mainly from Mont-St-Michel Bay, are offered *marinières* (with white wine, shallots, and herbs), or *à la St-Malo* (with cream).

Farm Produce

The Ceinture Dorée (Gold Belt), close to the coast, produces early vegetables in great quantities: artichokes, cauliflowers, peas, cabbages, potatoes, and onions. They enhance the distinctive taste of salt-meadow lamb (*pré-salé*), very much appreciated by gourmets. Brittany also has an abundance of locally reared chickens and ducks, from the Rennes and Nantes areas respectively, which form the basic ingredients of some delicious recipes. There are no great names in Breton cheeses, but you can find fresh local cheeses on market stalls and, to finish a meal, what could be closer to paradise than a bowl of Plougastel strawberries or Fouesnant cherries?

The Best of Breton Cuisine

Restaurants will nearly always include a seafood starter: oysters or mussels, crab or lobster with mayonnaise, as well as a variety of other shellfish. Enjoy it with a Muscadet, a light fruity white wine from the Loire region. The *cotriade*, a traditional fish soup, is an interesting alternative. For those who don't care for seafood, Breton *charcuterie* (cold sliced meats) will be a pleasant surprise.

Main dishes include the famous *homard à l'Armoricaine* (not 'l'Américaine'), lobster in a superb sauce of tomatoes, garlic and cognac; *gigot à la Bretonne*, lamb served with haricot beans; and *poulet au cidre*, chicken pieces cooked in cider and served with sautéed apples.

Desserts traditionally consist of *kouign-amann*, a rich cake made with lots of butter and caramelised sugar, or a lighter and quite pleasant prune flan

called *far*. A small glass of *chouchen*, distilled from honey, adds the finishing touch to a traditional Breton meal.

Food in Store
From speciality shops to hypermarkets, you're bound to come across unfamiliar items. Be bold! Culinary adventures aren't restricted to restaurants. Try that can of *ratatouille* or *cassoulet*, those intriguing-looking sausages, that pungent cheese the French women are asking for, the curious condiments that line the shelves, that packet of folded *crêpes*, and all those biscuits with strange names and shapes.

Taste the real, everyday France with an open mind and your experience will be that bit more authentic.

Tiers of temptation for lovers of shellfish are displayed at restaurants along Brittany's quays

Where to Eat

As everywhere in France, the choice of restaurants is wide and the decision hard to make, especially in tourist areas or main towns, where a whole string of establishments displays mouth-watering menus.

There are basically two types of restaurants: traditional and *crêperies*. As their name indicates, *crêperies* offer a complete range of *galettes* (savoury *crêpes*) as a main dish, served with a salad if you wish, and *crêpes de froment* (sweet *crêpes*) as a dessert. Such a meal, including a bottle of cider, is quite reasonable and a great favourite with children – that's why *crêperies* are often crowded.

Considering that meal times are roughly noon to 1.30pm and 7.30 to 9.30pm, it's worth booking a table at popular places.

Restaurants range from the village café or the quayside restaurant to the exclusive gastronomic establishment of a fashionable resort. Bear in mind that it's

Casual al fresco lunch outside a *crêperie*

usually much cheaper to choose a set-price menu than to choose the same number of à la carte courses. Moderately priced restaurants often advertise a cheap menu at lunch-time that is not available in the evening.

The star rating indicates the price of an average three-course meal in Euros, including service (*service compris*) but excluding drinks.

★   up to €17
★★   from €17 to €35
★★★   from €35 to €55
★★★★ over €55

St-Malo's rue Jacques-Cartier abounds with restaurants to suit all appetites

RENNES AND THE EAST
Chateaugiron
L'Aubergade ★★★
A 16th-century house close to the castle; refined cuisine using local produce.
2 rue Pierre et Julien Gourdel.
Tel: 02 99 37 41 35.

Dinan
Chez la Mère Pourcel ★★
A lovely Gothic house in the walled town; grilled artichoke cakes with *foie gras* a speciality.
3 place des Merciers.
Tel: 02 96 39 03 80.
La Caravelle ★★★
Elegant surroundings decorated with paintings; refined cuisine, poultry a speciality.
14 place Duclos.
Tel: 02 96 39 00 11.
Le Relais des Corsaires ★★★
A beautiful Renaissance house by the river; lots of atmosphere, seafood and fresh local produce.
3 rue du Quai, le Port.
Tel: 02 96 39 40 17.

Dol-de-Bretagne
Grand Hôtel de la Gare ★★
Wine and dine in the *belle époque* interior; specialities include a huge range of seafood, and lamb dishes.
21 ave Aristide Briand.
Tel: 02 99 48 00 44.

Hédé
Le Vieux Moulin ★★
Romantic setting; the regional cuisine includes a special fillet of duck with honeyed apples.
Ancienne route de St-Malo.
Tel: 02 99 45 45 70.

Rennes
Auberge St-Sauveur ★★★
Half-timbered house in the old town; traditional cuisine, fish and shellfish.
6 rue St-Sauveur.
Tel: 02 99 79 32 56.
Le Palais ★★
Close to the beautiful Palais de Justice; tasty local dishes according to availability of fresh produce.
7 place du Parlement de Bretagne.
Tel: 02 99 79 45 01.
Le Piré ★★★★
In a wooded park right in the town centre; gourmet cuisine.
23 rue du Maréchal Joffre.
Tel: 02 99 79 31 41.

NORTHERN BRITTANY
Cancale
Maison de Bricourt ★★★★
In the town centre, with fresh oysters and lamb specialities .
1 rue du Guesclin.
Tel: 02 99 89 64 76.

Dinard
La Vallée ★★★
Specialities fish, lobster and other shellfish.
6 ave George V.
Tel: 02 99 46 94 00.

Mûr-de-Bretagne
Auberge Grand Maison ★★★
Near Guerlédan lake; top-quality chef and warm welcome.
1 rue Léon le Cerf.
Tel: 02 96 28 51 10.

Paimpol
Crêperie de l'Abbaye de Beauport ★
Conveniently close to the ruins of the abbey.
32 rue de Beauport, Kérity Paimpol.
Tel: 02 96 20 80 21.

Ploumanac'h
Hôtel des Rochers ★★★★
Overlooking Ploumanac'h harbour with wonderful views of the pink granite; gourmet cuisine, specialities grilled lobster and crêpe Nanou. Advance booking essential.
Port de Ploumanac'h.
Tel: 02 96 91 44 49.

St-Brieuc
Le Ribeault ★
Crêperie; speciality *crêpes flambé.*
10 rue Fardel.
Tel: 02 96 33 44 79.

St-Malo
Crêperie Solidor ★
A charming and friendly place to enjoy *crêpes* and *galettes.*
7 esplanade du Colt Menguy, Solidor.
Tel: 02 99 81 64 53.
La Duchesse Anne ★★★
In the walled town at the foot of the ramparts; specialities are lobster and fish.
5 place Guy-la-Chambre.
Tel: 02 99 40 85 33.
La Corderie ★★
A very calm place with a view of the sea.
Reasonable prices.

Chemin de la Corderie, St Servan.
Tel: 02 99 81 62 38.

St-Quay-Portrieux
Crêperie de la Plage ★★
Near the beach, open seven days a week.
7 place de la Plage.
Tel: 02 96 70 49 93.

Le Val-André
Domaine du Val ★★★
Stately mansion; specialities lobster *à l'Armoricaine*, home-made *foie gras.*
Planguenoual.
Tel: 02 96 32 75 40.

FINISTÈRE
Audierne
Le Bar Bretou ★★
Mainly fish restaurant.
2 quai Jacques de Thézac.
Tel: 02 98 70 10 95.

Bénodet
La Ferme du Letty ★★★
Close to the lagoon, rustic decor, warm welcome; varied cuisine.
Le Letty, Bénodet.
Tel: 02 98 57 01 27.
L'Agape ★★
In Ste-Marine opposite Bénodet, cosy atmos-phere; seafood a speciality.
52 rue de la Plage, Ste-Marine.
Tel: 02 98 56 32 70.

Concarneau
La Coquille ★★
In the fishing harbour; interesting decor with antique furniture and paintings.
Quai du Moro.
Tel: 02 98 97 08 52.

Douarnez
Le Tristan ★★
In the harbour with sea view, many paintings.
25 bis rue du Rosmeur.
Tel: 02 98 92 20 17.

Fouesnant-Beg Meil
Thalamot ★★★
At Pointe de Beg-Meil, close to beaches, 1930s' decor with paintings by Fredriksen; specialities fillet of duck cooked with apples and cider; seafood.
4/6 le Chemin Creux.
Tel: 02 98 94 97 38.

Vannes' place Gambetta, with shaded tables where travellers can sit and watch the world go by

Pont-Aven
Moulin de Rosmadec ★★★
A 15th-century beamed watermill on the banks of the Aven; justifiably famed food.
Pont-Aven.
Tel: 02 98 06 00 22.

Quimper
Crêperie de Locmaria ★
Near HB Henriot ceramic factory.
Route de Bénodet.
Tel: 02 98 52 06 64.
L'Ambroisie ★★★
Close to the cathedral, contemporary decor; gourmet cuisine.
49 rue Elie Fréron.
Tel: 02 98 95 00 02.
La Krampouzerie ★
Crêperie in old Quimper.
Place au Beurre.
Tel: 02 98 95 13 08.
Le Grand Café de Bretagne ★★
On the embankment; *crêpes*, grilled meat, seafood.
18 rue du Parc.
Tel: 02 98 95 00 13.

Ste-Anne-La-Palud
Restaurant de la Plage ★★★★
Magnificent seaview; speciality, as is expected, is seafood.
On the beach.
Tel: 02 98 92 50 12.

St-Guenolé
Restaurant de la Mer ★★★
Near the famous rock formations; speciality fish and seafood.
184 rue François Péron.
Tel: 02 98 58 62 22.

SOUTHERN BRITTANY
Auray
Restaurant de l'Abbaye ★★
Half-timbered house in the old St-Goustan quarter, specialities grilled lobster and stuffed crab.
19 place St-Sauveur.
Tel: 02 97 24 10 85.

Hennebont
Château de Locguénolé ★★★★
Hotel on east bank of Blavet between Hennebont and Port-Louis, vast park; gourmet cuisine.
Route de Port-Louis.
Tel: 02 97 76 76 76.

Nantes
La Cigale ★★
Art Nouveau style in the centre of 19th-century Nantes. Good seafood lunches and cakes.
4 place Graslin.
Tel: 02 51 84 94 94.
La Reine Margot ★★
At the heart of old Nantes, rustic decor; traditional cooking

(closed August).
8 rue de la Juiverie.
Tel: 02 40 47 43 85.
Le Gavroche ★★★
Terrace, parking; gourmet cuisine.
139 rue des Hauts-Pavés.
Tel: 02 40 76 22 49.

Questembert
Le Bretagne ★★★★
Sophisticated decor; refined cuisine.
Rue St-Michel.
Tel: 02 97 26 11 12.

La Roche-Bernard
Auberge Bretonne ★★★
One of Brittany's most attractive restaurants with a highly original interior; imaginative chef.
2 place du Guesclin.
Tel: 02 99 90 60 28.

Vannes
La Morgate ★★
17th-century house east of the old town; specialities fish, and grilled lobster.
21 rue de la Fontaine.
Tel: 02 97 42 42 39.
Restaurant de Roscanvec ★★
Situated in the old pedestrian district, it offers a superb spread of traditional cuisine by a young chef.
17 rue des Halles.
Tel: 02 97 47 15 96.

Crêpes and Cider

Pancakes are undoubtedly the most famous product of Breton cuisine. Now elevated to a real art, *crêpes* are celebrated every July – with the requisite music and dancing – in Gourin, in the depths of Montagnes Noires country.

What is the secret of *crêpes'* universal appeal? They are, after all, only thin pancakes – or are they? To this conundrum every Breton will give a slightly different but equally passionate response, from which one may deduce that it is all a question of know-how (due must be given to Breton pride) and of versatility (and homage paid to Breton imagination)!

There are basically two kinds of *crêpes* – or rather, *crêpe* is the name of one of the two kinds, the other being called *galette*. The main difference is the

type of flour used: *galettes* are made with buckwheat flour, an ancient cereal that had totally disappeared from Breton fields and is now making a comeback. *Crêpes*, on the other hand, are made with wheat flour.

Galettes are served with a great variety of savoury fillings – cheese, ham, bacon, egg, seafood, onions, mushrooms etc – while the lighter *crêpes* are enhanced by hot chocolate sauce, ice cream, Grand Marnier, honey, and fruit, to name but a few mouth-watering possibilities.

You cannot fully appreciate the subtle taste of a good pancake without a *bolée de cidre* (mug of cider) or, better still, cider from Fouesnant in south Cornouaille where an apple festival is held in July. Like wine, cider varies from year to year, and there are different types according to sugar content. *Crêperies* usually give you the choice between *cidre brut,* very slightly sweet, suitable for savoury *crêpes*, and *cidre doux*, sweet and frothy with a low alcohol content, suitable for desserts.

Cider is widely used in cooking fish, seafood, poultry, meat and desserts. Distilled, it becomes a strong alcohol called *lambig* which is drunk with coffee after a meal. Cider is also used to make up cocktails; here is the recipe of a very refreshing summer drink: 1 part *sirop de framboise* (raspberry concentrate), 1 part *lambig*, 6 parts cool *cidre brut*. Cheers!

You're never far from a *crêperie* in Brittany (facing page below) where you can start with a savoury *galette*, or snack on *crêpes* in the market (above); the cider museum in Argol (facing page above)

Hotels and Accommodation

Accommodation of every sort is available. Simple family hotels, luxury establishments at fashionable resorts, delightful privately-owned châteaux, cosy thatched cottages, rustic *gîtes ruraux*, friendly farms, well-appointed campsites, even functional youth hostels – you name it, Brittany has it.

Les Portes Rouges Hotel in Cancale

Theme Holidays

The choice of theme holidays is now so wide that price alone is no longer the deciding factor. More and more holidaymakers, taking suggestions from professionals, are turning to theme holiday formulas that combine a hobby or a sport with the discovery of a region, meanwhile remaining as free as they wish. Personalised planning is undertaken for you by people who know the area very well, a service particularly valuable for first-time visitors.

Among Brittany's numerous possibilities are hiking, cycling, and riding tours (with or without guides) around a nature theme in remote parts of the region. Typically, detailed itineraries are provided, hotels or other accommodation booked in advance, and transport of luggage organised.

There are also sailing trips for beginners or experienced yachtsmen, along the coast or around the islands; fishing trips to the best fishing grounds in the Channel and the Atlantic; kayak trips round the Côte de Granit Rose; golf tours of the most famous golf courses; keep-fit holidays in hydrotherapy centres, and many more. For detailed information and reservations, ring **Bretagne Infos** (*tel: 02 99 36 15 15*), or contact the following:

Comité Départemental du Tourisme du Finistère, 11 rue Théodore-Le-Hars, BP 1419, 29104 Quimper Cedex. *Tel: 02 98 76 20 70.*

Formules Bretagne, Maison de la Bretagne, 203 bd Saint-Germain, 75007 Paris. *Tel: 01 53 63 11 50.*

Comité Départemental du Tourisme des Côtes d'Armor, 7 rue Saint-Benoît, 22000 St-Brieuc. *Tel: 02 96 62 72 00.*

Comité Départemental du Tourisme (Ille-et-Vilaine), 4 rue Jean Jaurès, 35000 Rennes. *Tel: 02 99 78 47 47.*

Comité Départemental du Tourisme du Loire-Atlantique, 2 allée Baco, 44000 Nantes. *Tel: 02 51 72 95 30.*

Comité Départemental du Tourisme du Morbihan, allée Nicolas Le Blanc, 5600 Vannes. *Tel: 02 97 54 06 56.*

Hotels

Brittany's thousand or so hotels are renowned for their warm welcome, which can be partly explained by the fact that a large number of them are family run.

Some hotels, particularly in the smaller resorts, are only open during the season, so it's well worth checking such details during the planning stage. The Comité Régional du Tourisme de Bretagne publishes a brochure entitled *Hôtels* where opening times are given, together with prices and grading.

Room-only rates, inclusive of service, are for two people sharing; but half-board (*demi-pension*) rates are per person based on two people sharing a room (*chambre*). Always check prices directly with the hotel when booking, as they're liable to change. If your heart is set on going to a highly popular resort along the coast during the high season,

then you'd do well to book at least four months in advance.

Hotels are graded as follows:
4-star: luxury hotel
3-star: very comfortable hotel
2-star: good average hotel
1-star: plain but fairly comfortable hotel
RT: hotel/residence (possibility of self-catering)
SE: classified hotel without star.

Several well-known chains of hotels, such as Relais et Châteaux, Best Western and Sofitel, have establishments in Brittany.

A useful regional association that includes nearly 300 hotels/ restaurants is the **Fédération Bretonne des Logis de France**, BP 94, 35 413 St-Malo Cedex *(tel: 02 99 81 31 46)*.

A sweeping drive leads to luxury accommodation in the chic seaside resort of Dinard

The ultimate fresh-air experience: camping in the sea breezes of Rothéneuf

Châteaux

The Châteaux et Demeures de l'Ouest are not hotels but private residences whose owners welcome a limited number of guests within their family circle. A brochure entitled *Bienvenue au Château* is available from the Comité Régional de Tourisme de Bretagne (*see* Tourist Information, *p189*).

Farms and Chambres d'Hôtes

Farm holidays are increasingly popular. Guests can have meals with the farmer and his family, who are only too pleased to share their love and knowledge of the area.

Chambres d'hôtes is the French equi-valent of B & B; some places even provide full board. Those selected by the *départements'* tourist authorities for the quality of their amenities and of their welcome are entitled to be called *Gîtes de France*, and these are graded into four categories (called *épis*), according to certain criteria. For instance, in order to belong to the highest categories – three and four *épis* – rooms must have an en-suite bathroom and toilet. Breakfast is copious and usually includes home-made produce.

For detailed information contact:

Gîtes de France, 42 ave du Président-

The oft seen sign of farmhouse B & B

Wilson, 56400 Auray. *Tel: 02 97 56 48 12.*
Gîtes de France, 1 allée Baco, 44000
Nantes. *Tel: 02 51 72 95 65.*
Gîtes de France-Accueil Rural,
Finistère Maison de l'Agriculture,
5 allée de Sully, 29322 Quimper Cedex.
Tel: 02 98 64 20 20.
Gîtes de France, Côtes d'Armor, 5 rue
Saint-Benoît, 22000 St-Brieuc.
Tel: 02 96 62 21 70.

Self-catering

Total freedom and a closer contact with
the local population are the main
advantages of self-catering. Standards,
however, vary markedly, and their
assessment from a distance is difficult.
Tourist authorities have therefore
established a grading system called *Nids
Vacances* based on well-defined, carefully
checked criteria; there are one to four
nids (nests). The **Comité Régional du
Tourisme de Bretagne** (*see address in*
Practical Guide, *p189*) publishes a
brochure called *Locations Bretagne*,
which lists a selection of the main estate
agents dealing with holiday rentals.

Résidences hôtelières combine the
freedom of self-catering with the usual
services available in hotels.

Gîtes ruraux are a category apart:
country holiday houses which, like the
Gîtes de France, are graded from one to
four *épis*.

Camping

Apart from campsites allowed on
farmland under certain conditions, all
places are graded into four categories
with one to four stars – and there are
roughly a thousand of them in Brittany.
Some top-class campsites have formed

associations to draw the tourists'
attention to their similar excellent
amenities.

The **Fédération Française de
Camping-Caravaning** can be contacted
at 78 rue de Rivoli, 75004 Paris,
(*tel: 01 42 72 84 08*).

Youth Hostels

Access to the 30 *auberges de jeunesse*
(youth hostels) in Brittany is reserved
for members of the Fédération Unie
des Auberges de Jeunesse, 27 rue Pajol,
75018 Paris (*tel: 01 44 89 87 27*).

Practical information is provided by
the Comité Départemental de Tourisme
of each département (*see p189 for
addresses*).

Pitching a tent in St-Malo's City Fort, now a
campsite

On Business

Whether you're planning an individual business trip, a seminar, or a conference, professional agencies at your destination can save you time and ensure that everything goes smoothly. They take care of everything: booking hotels and conference premises, planning work sessions, catering, suggesting leisure activities, and receptions.

Fast TGV connections have improved Brittany's business prospects

Below are names of recognised agencies:

Agri Pass
Specialists in agriculture and fishing.
BP 190, 29204 Morlaix Cedex.
Tel: 02 98 63 22 11; fax: 02 98 63 36 62.

Atlantica International
CP 30 – Le Prisme II, Parc d'Innovation de Bretagne Sud, 56038 Vannes Cedex.
Tel: 02 97 68 14 30; fax: 02 97 68 14 18;
www.atlantigroupes.com

Séminor
Office de Tourisme du Pays de Lorient, quai de Rohan, Maison de la Mer, 56100 Lorient. Tel: 02 97 21 00 52; fax: 02 97 21 06 65.

Voyages en Bretagne
44 rue Emile Zola, 29200 Brest.
Tel: 02 98 44 41 00; fax: 02 98 43 22 95.

When planning a business trip, remember that working hours include a 2-hour lunch break from noon to 2pm, during which administrative offices are closed.

Most French business men and women speak English, but they will appreciate your effort to greet them in French, then continue talking in English anyway if it's easier for all concerned.

Travelling

Brittany is easily accessible by fast TGV (*train à grande vitesse*) from Paris (2 hours to Rennes) and by road on the A11 motorway from Paris (3 hours to Rennes). There are direct flights from many European cities to the international airports of Rennes St-Jacques and Nantes Atlantique and internal flights from Dinard, St-Brieuc, Brest, Quimper and Lorient.

Within Brittany, travelling times are being steadily reduced by the gradual extension of the TGV lines and of the dual-carriageway network.

Most international car-hire companies are represented:

Nantes
Avis, Gare SNCF. Tel: 02 40 89 25 50.

Quimper
Europcar, 16 av. de la Libération.
Tel: 02 98 90 00 68.

Rennes
Avis, Pl. de la Gare. Tel: 02 23 42 14 14.

St-Brieuc
Hertz, 53 rue de la Gare.
Tel: 02 96 94 25 89.

Hotels

Many hotels now specialise in welcoming business people, either individually or in groups. In addition to what you might reasonably expect, specialised hotels offer car hire, currency exchange, detailed tourist information, and transfer to and from the station or airport. Credits cards most widely accepted are VISA, American Express, and Diners International.

Communications

Equipment available on the premises include a typewriter, telefax, television and video recorder, photocopying machine, and slide projector. Secretarial and translation services are available on request. The minitel, a computer terminal linked to a telephone line, that can also be linked to a printer and used as a fax machine, is standard equipment.

Bookings

A list of hotels is available on request.

Write to the **Comité Régional du Tourisme de Bretagne** (1 rue Raoul Ponchon, 35000 Rennes), or contact Bretagne Infos (*tel: 02 99 36 15 15*).

Seminars and Conferences

A brochure entitled *Séminaires Incentive* is available from the Comité Régional du Tourisme de Bretagne. It contains a choice of hotels with suitable facilities, as well as details on three large conference centres, including the brand-new Palais du Grand Large in St-Malo, the Quartz in Brest, or the Palais des Congrès in Lorient.

An interesting option is conducting seminars or business meetings aboard traditional sailing ships – an impressive and unusual way of combining business with pleasure.

Rennes airport, with direct flights from London

Practical Guide

Arriving
EU residents visiting France need only a valid passport; so do US, Canadian and New Zealand citizens, provided the length of their stay does not exceed three months. They need a visa for longer stays and Australians need a visa whatever their length of stay. Visas are obtainable from French embassies and consulates in your own country; to be on the safe side, allow two months to receive it.

By Sea
Brittany Ferries has regular year-round sailings to St-Malo from Portsmouth, Poole and Cork, and to Roscoff from Plymouth and Cork; sailings to Normandy are to Caen from Portsmouth and to Cherbourg from Poole.

By Air
Brittany is well-connected by air to the rest of Europe with many airlines offering convenient low-cost flights. There are also direct flights from Paris to Rennes, St-Brieuc, Brest, Quimper, and Lorient, from London to Rennes, Brest and Dinard (via the Channel Islands); and from Cork to Brest and Quimper. Nantes airport has direct links with most important European cities.

By Rail
The *Thomas Cook European Timetable*, published monthly and giving up-to-date details of most rail services and many shipping services throughout Europe, will help you plan a rail journey to, from and around France. It is

available in the UK from some stations, offices of Thomas Cook, or by phoning *(44) 1733 416477*. In the USA, contact the Forsyth Travel Library, Westchester 1, 44 South Broadway, White Plains, New York 1060; *tel: (914) 681 7250; toll-free tel: 1 800 367 7984; fax: (914) 681 7251.*

Rennes and Nantes are only 2 hours from Paris by the fast TGV (*train à grande vitesse*) which reaches Brest, the westernmost town in Brittany, in four hours.

By Car
At le Mans the A11 motorway connects with the A81 to Rennes, while the A11 continues to Nantes: both cities can be reached in about 3 hours from Paris. A convenient network of fast dual carriageways links most Breton cities: the N12 along the north coast, the N165 along the south coast, and the north-south N137 St-Malo/Rennes/Nantes.

Camping
See p179.

Children
Most hotels in holiday resorts put up extra beds for children in their parents' room on request and some offer a babysitting service. But the **Gîtes de France** (*see pp178–9*) are a particularly suitable type of accommodation for children, as they offer more freedom and many have outdoor games, bikes, ponies, and babysitters at hand.

Some restaurants advertise a special children's menu but most will make up a simple dish on request (provided the place isn't too busy) or heat up food in jars or cans that you provide – handy when your toddler will only eat ravioli! Babyfood and nappies are cheaper in hypermarkets (*see p150*).

Climate

Brittany's climate is mild, with maximum temparatures between 20°C and 25°C in July and August. The weather is changeable, however, so clothing should range from beachwear to light pullovers and rainwear.

Conversion Tables

See p185.
Clothes and shoe sizes in Brittany generally follow the standard sizes used in the Rest of Europe.

Crime

Petty theft is a nuisance. Never leave

valuables, such as cameras and golf clubs, visible inside a parked car, particularly in large towns. When you go to the beach, avoid taking money and credit cards and if that cannot be avoided, never leave your belongings unattended on the sand. Pickpockets are on the lookout in market-day crowds and in busy streets during *pardons* and festivals. Watch your wallet and your bag carefully.

Weather Conversion Chart
25.4mm = 1 inch
°F = 1.8 x °C + 32

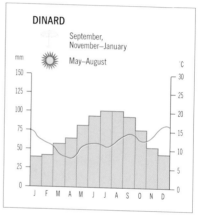

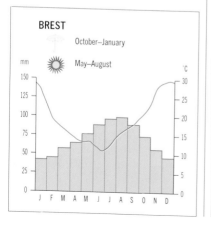

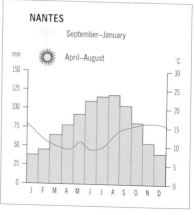

Driving

Make sure you take your car registration
papers and driving licence. You must
have a current insurance certificate (plus
a letter of authorisation if the vehicle is
not registered in your name). International Insurance Certificates (Green
Cards) are no longer compulsory, but
you are advised to apply for one if you
want fully comprehensive cover.

White headlights are now officially
accepted. Front and rear seat belts
should be worn at all times. Road signs
are international and speed limits range
from 50km/h in built-up areas unless
otherwise indicated, to 90km/h on
ordinary roads, 110km/h on dual
carriageways and 130km/h on motor-
ways. Speed limits are lower by 10 to
20km/h in wet conditions.

Traffic in France drives on the right.
The *priorité à droite* (giving way to
traffic approaching from the right) is
strictly observed in built-up areas and at
crossroads where no right of way is
indicated, but not at roundabouts.

Parking in town centres is usually
restricted; tickets for up to 2 hours are
available from distributors.

There are 4 grades of fuel: *gasoil* or
gazole (diesel), *super* (98 octane), *sans
plomb* (95 octane unleaded), and *super
sans plomb* (98 octane unleaded). Petrol
is cheapest at hypermarkets and dearest
on motor-ways.

There are car-hire companies in most
towns; ask for a list at the local tourist
office.

Electricity

220 volts. Electric sockets take plugs
with two round pins.

Embassies

Australia
4 rue Jean Rey, 75015 Paris.
Tel: 01 40 59 33 00.

Canada
35 avenue Montaigne, 75008 Paris.
Tel: 01 44 43 29 00.

Ireland
4 rue Rude, 75016 Paris.
Tel: 01 44 17 67 00.

New Zealand
7 ter rue Léonard de Vinci, 75016 Paris.
Tel: 01 45 01 43 43.

UK
5 rue du Faubourg-St-Honoré, 75008
Paris. *Tel: 01 44 51 31 00.*

USA
2 avenue Gabriel, 75008 Paris.
Tel: 01 43 12 22 22.

Emergency Telephone Numbers

There are three main emergency
telephone numbers operating
throughout France:
Ambulance (*Samu*) 15.
Fire (*Pompiers*) 18.
Police (*Police secours*) 17.

Health

There are no mandatory vaccination
requirements. It is recommended that
travellers keep tetanus and polio
immunisation up to date. Like every
other part of the world, AIDS is present.
Food and water are safe.

EU residents should get form E111
from health authorities in their own
country, which entitles them to the same
benefits as French nationals, that is, the
reimbursement of about 70 per cent of
medical expenses. They are advised to
get separate medical insurance available

from motoring organisations and travel agencies. For residents outside the EU, cover varies according to their health insurance policy at home. They should get the relevant information from their own company.

Lost Property

Enquire at the local *gendarmerie*.

Media
Newspapers

The most popular newspaper is *Ouest-France*, but all the national papers are on sale in the *maisons de la presse* (newsagents). International newspapers are on sale in large towns and in most holiday resorts during the high season.

Television and Radio

There are six channels on French television. In addition, France can receive foreign channels via satellite. Among the national radio stations, France Infos is a non-stop news programme, France Musique deals exclusively with music, and France Inter is a mixed programme of topical, cultural and light entertainment. There are also many local stations. Holiday news in English is broadcast on Radio France Bretagne Ouest, on 93 FM at 10am and 5pm.

The BBC World Service is available on medium wave/AM at 648kHz, and Radio 4 on long wave at 198kHz.

Money Matters

As in the rest of France, the Euro (€) is the unit of currency used in Brittany. There are seven denominations of the Euro note: €5, €10, €20, €50, €100,

Conversion Table

FROM	TO	MULTIPLY BY
Inches	Centimetres	2.54
Feet	Metres	0.3048
Yards	Metres	0.9144
Miles	Kilometres	1.6090
Acres	Hectares	0.4047
Gallons	Litres	4.5460
Ounces	Grams	28.35
Pounds	Grams	453.6
Pounds	Kilograms	0.4536
Tons	Tonnes	1.0160

To convert back, for example from centimetres to inches, divide by the number in the third column.

Men's Suits

UK	36	38	40	42	44	46	48
Rest of Europe	46	48	50	52	54	56	58
USA	36	38	40	42	44	46	48

Dress Sizes

UK	8	10	12	14	16	18
France	36	38	40	42	44	46
Italy	38	40	42	44	46	48
Rest of Europe	34	36	38	40	42	44
USA	6	8	10	12	14	16

Men's Shirts

UK	14	14.5	15	15.5	16	16.5	17
Rest of Europe	36	37	38	39/40	41	42	43
USA	14	14.5	15	15.5	16	16.5	17

Men's Shoes

UK	7	7.5	8.5	9.5	10.5	11
Rest of Europe	41	42	43	44	45	46
USA	8	8.5	9.5	10.5	11.5	12

Women's Shoes

UK	4.5	5	5.5	6	6.5	7
Rest of Europe	38	38	39	39	40	41
USA	6	6.5	7	7.5	8	8.5

€200, and €500; eight denominations of coins: 1 cent, 2 cents, 5 cents, 10 cents, 20 cents, 50 cents, and €1 and €2.

Currency can be exchanged in banks and in some hotels. Some shops also accept traveller's cheques. Outside banks, there are numerous cash dispensers that accept foreign cards and give instructions in four different languages including English. Rather than carry large amounts of money, you can pay by credit card almost everywhere.

Traveller's Cheques denominated in Euros are recommended, though cheques in US dollars are accepted.

National Holidays

Administrative offices, banks, some museums and sights, and most shops are closed on national holidays. Some hypermarkets and local shops stay open.

1 January New Year's Day
April, variable Easter Monday
1 May May Day
8 May Victory Day (1945)
May, variable Ascension Day
May, variable Whit Monday
14 July Bastille Day
15 August Feast of the Assumption
1 November All Saints' Day
11 November Armistice Day
25 December Christmas Day

Opening Hours

Banks open from 9am to 4.30 or 5pm, closing on Sunday plus either Saturday or Monday, depending on market day. Shops usually open from 9am to 7pm except Sunday. Food shops often open on Sunday morning. A lot of shops close between noon and 2pm. Many

LANGUAGE

Quite a few people speak Breton, but everyone speaks French.

COMMON BRETON WORDS

aber	estuary
argoat	inland, wooded area
armor	coastline
beg	point
bihan	small
bras	large
Breizh	Brittany
castel	castle
fest-noz	night feast
ker	village, hamlet
lan	church
loc	monastery
menez	mountain
meur	large, important
penn	head, tip, summit
plou	parish
porz	port
roc'h	rock
ros	mound, hill
ti	house
tro	valley

BASIC FRENCH WORDS AND PHRASES

yes	oui
no	non
please	s'il vous plaît
thank you	merci
excuse me	excusez-moi
I'm sorry	pardon
good morning	bonjour
good evening	bonsoir
goodnight	bonne nuit
goodbye	au revoir
I have . . .	J'ai . . .
It is . . .	C'est . . .

Do you speak English?	Parlez-vous anglais?	**to eat**	manger
I do not understand	Je ne comprends pas	**to drink**	boire
		menu	la carte
Could you speak more slowly please?	Pouvez-vous parler plus lentement s'il vous plaît?	**starters**	les hors d'oeuvre
		meat	la viande
		rare	saignant
		well-done	bien cuit
I would like . . .	Je voudrais . . .	**fish**	le poisson
when	quand	**seafood**	les fruits de mer
yesterday	hier	**vegetables**	les légumes
today	aujourd'hui	**chips**	des frites
tomorrow	demain	**salt/pepper**	du sel/poivre
At what time . . ?	A quelle heure . . ?	**bread**	du pain
here	ici	**butter**	du beurre
there	là	**cheese**	du fromage
near	près	**wine list**	la carte des vins
before	avant	**red/white**	rouge/blanc
in front of	devant	**water**	de l'eau
behind	derrière	**coffee**	un café
opposite	en face de	**white**	au lait
right	à droite	**beer**	de la bière
left	à gauche	**cider**	du cidre
straight on	tout droit	**tea with milk**	un thé au lait
road	la route	**Waiter!**	Monsieur!
motorway	l'autoroute	**Waitress!**	Mademoiselle!
dual carriageway	la voie express	**Where are the toilets?**	Où sont les toilettes?
bridge	le pont	**Can I have the bill?**	L'addition s'il vous plaît
street	la rue		
garage/petrol station	la station service	**shop**	le magasin
		market	le marché
My car has broken down	Ma voiture est en panne	**open**	ouvert
		closed	fermé
railway station	la gare	**money**	l'argent
		notes	des billets
platform	le quai	**traveller's cheques**	des chèques de voyage
a ticket for . . .	un billet pour . . .		
harbour	le port	**How much is this?**	Combien coûte ceci?
airport	l'aéroport		
flight to . . .	le vol à destination de . . .	**May I have a receipt?**	Puis-je avoir un reçu?
I am looking for . . .	Je cherche . . .		
(hotel, castle, etc)	(l'hôtel, le château, etc)		

are closed on Monday morning unless it's market day. Hypermarkets often stay open late one or two nights a week; they close on Sunday. Museums' opening times vary according to the season.

Organised Tours

Check the brochures published by the Comité Départemental de Tourisme, which has offices in each *département*. There are more details and addresses in *Theme Holidays* (*see p176*).

For all information contact Bretagne Infos (*tel: 02 99 36 15 15*).

Pharmacies

Pharmacies are closed on Sunday and sometimes on Saturday afternoon. All pharmacy doors display a list of on-duty chemists, called *pharmacies de garde*.

Places of Worship

For your nearest place of worship, contact your local tourist office.

Police

Police duties are carried out by the Gendarmerie Nationale. In the country, gendarmes patrol highways, while in town they control traffic, but in both cases they deal with crime as well.

Post Offices

Bureaux de poste are open Monday to Friday 9am–6pm, with a lunch break in small villages, and Saturday 9am–noon. Street signs near the town centre often point to the local PTT.

Post boxes are yellow, freestanding, or set into a wall. You can receive poste restante mail anywhere, as long as it is clearly addressed to you, *Poste Restante*, with the name and postal code of the village or town. Stamps can also be bought in a *tabac* (tobacconist).

Public Transport

Regular internal flights connect major towns and islands like Ouessant and Belle-Ile.

Rail links between Rennes, Nantes, and other major towns are complemented by a network of coach services listed in the Guide TER, available from the Comité Régional du Tourisme (*see p189*) or the Direction Régionale SNCF (22 boulevard Beaumont, BP 2022, 35040 Rennes Cedex).

There are boat services to the main islands round the coast (*for details see local tourist offices*).

Main towns offer bus and taxi services; for route plans see local tourist offices.

Senior Citizens

All senior citizens are allowed a discount on entrance fees to sights and museums. They may be asked to show their passports.

Student and Youth Travel

See Youth Hostels, *p179*.

Telephones

Some public telephones are still coin-operated, but the majority work on a *télécarte* (phone card) of 50 or 120 units, sold at post offices and tobacconists. To direct-dial an international call, dial *00* (wait for dial tone) + country code (**Australia** *61*, **Canada** *1*, **Ireland** *353*, **New Zealand** *64*, **UK** *44*, **USA** *1*) + area code (leave out any initial *0*) + number.

To call via the operator, dial *00* (wait for dial tone) + *33*. For reverse-charge calls, dial: **Australia** *19 00 61*, **Canada** *19 00 16*, **New Zealand** *19 00 64*, **UK** *19 00 44*, **USA** *19 00 11* and *19 00 19*.

Calls from hotels are more expensive. International calls are cheaper after 7.30pm and on Saturday and Sunday.

Time

Summer: GMT +2; Winter: GMT +1. When it is noon in Brittany (winter time), it is: 9pm in Canberra, 11am in Dublin, 11am in London, 6am in Ottawa, 6am in Washington. and 11pm in Wellington.

Tipping

Service charges are included in restaurants and cafés, but it is customary to tip barmen, hotel porters and chambermaids, museum guides, usherettes in cinemas, hairdressers and taxi drivers.

Toilets

There are public toilets in commercial centres, hypermarkets, petrol stations, cafés, and restaurants. Smaller establishments sometimes have a single facility for both sexes.

Tourist Information

There are four levels of information centres:

National
Maison de la Bretagne, 203 boulevard Saint-Germain, 75007 Paris.
Tel: 01 53 63 11 50.

Regional
Comité Régional du Tourisme, 1 rue Raoul Ponchon, 35000 Rennes.
Tel: 02 99 36 15 15.

Departmental
Comité Départemental du Tourisme, located at:
2, allée Baco, 44000 Nantes.
Tel: 02 51 72 95 30.
11 rue Le Hars, BP 1419, 29104 Quimper Cedex. *Tel: 02 98 76 20 70.*
4 rue Jean Jaurès, 35000 Rennes.
Tel: 02 99 78 47 47.
7 rue Saint-Benôit, 22000 St-Brieuc.
Tel: 02 96 62 72 00.
Allée Nicolas Leblanc, 56000 Vannes.
Tel: 02 97 54 06 56.

Local
The list of local tourist offices can be found in all the brochures at regional and departmental level.

Travellers with Disabilities

For hotels and campsites see the official brochure *Hôtels and Campings Caravaning* published by the Comité Régional de Tourisme de Bretagne.

The Comité Départemental du Tourisme of each *département* publishes a guide listing easily accessible sights, available on request. For more general information about travelling in France, write to the **Association des Paralyses de France** (17 boulevard Auguste Blanqui, 75013 Paris, *tel: 01 40 78 69 00; www.apf.asso.fr*).

Cafés and restaurants in Rennes

ACKNOWLEDGEMENTS
Thomas Cook Publishing wishes to thank the following photographers, libraries and associations for their assistance in the preparation of this book.

NATURE PHOTOGRAPHERS (D Osborne) 144b
PICTURES COLOUR LIBRARY 13, 53, 59
SPECTRUM COLOUR LIBRARY 6, 18a, 48, 54, 102b, 116b, 145b, 180 & spine
MARY EVANS PICTURE LIBRARY 8
WERNER FORMAN ARCHIVES 12a, 12b
THE BRIDGEMAN ART LIBRARY 103
TRAVEL IMAGES 11

The remaining pictures (including back cover top right) are held in the AA PHOTO LIBRARY and were taken by:
RICK STRANGE with the exception of pages 1, 40, 41, 43, 44, 57, 83, 85, 120, 130, 133, 159a, 159b, 169, back cover top centre which were taken by A BAKER; pages 2, 7, 15, 21, 25, 28b, 63, 67, 69, 70, 80b, 82, 84, 91, 92, 104b, 114, 127, 129, 143, 149, 150, 151, 153, 158a, 164, 166, 174b, 174c, 178a, back cover cutout which were taken by ROY VICTOR; pages 4, 16, 26, 28a, 30, 32b, 33, 36, 38, 39, 58, 60, 61, 64, 71, 78, 148, 170, 171, 176, 177, 178b, 179, 181, 189, back cover top left which were taken by STEVE DAY; pages 24, 31, 34, 79, 88, 154, 155, 160, 162, 165 which were taken by BARRIE SMITH; and page 119 which was taken by R MOORE.

FOR LABURNUM TECHNOLOGIES

Design Director	Alpana Khare	**Photo Editor**	Manju Singhal
Series Director	Razia Grover	**DTP Designer**	Harish Aggarwal
Editors	Madhumadhavi Singh, Rajiv Jayaram	**CD Editor**	Arfin Zukof
Designer	Neeraj Aggarwal	**CD Designer**	Sudhir Horo

Updating and additional research on this edition was done by Paul Hines.
Thanks to Marie Lorimer for the Index.

Travellers

Feedback Form

Please help us improve future editions by taking part in our reader survey. Every returned form will be acknowledged. To show our appreciation we will send you a voucher entitling you to £1 off your next *Travellers* guide or any other Thomas Cook guidebook ordered direct from Thomas Cook Publishing. Just take a few minutes to complete and return this form to us.

We'd also be glad to hear of your comments, updates or recommendations on places we cover or you think that we ought to cover.

1. Which *Travellers* guide did you purchase?

_____

2. Have you purchased other *Travellers* guides in the series?

Yes ☐

No ☐

If Yes, please specify_____

3. Which of the following tempted you into buying your *Travellers* guide: (Please tick as many as appropriate)

The price ☐

The FREE weblinks CD ☐

The cover ☐

The content ☐

Other_____

4. What do you think of :

a) the cover design? _____

b) the design and layout styles within the book?_____

c) the FREE weblinks CD?_____

5. Please tell us about any features that in your opinion could be changed, improved or added in future editions of the book or CD:

_____

_____

Your age category: ☐ under 21   ☐ 21-30   ☐ 31-40   ☐ 41-50   ☐ 51+

Mr/Mrs/Miss/Ms/Other

Surname_____ Initials_____

Full address: (Please include postal or zip code)_____

_____

Daytime telephone number: _____

Email address: _____

☐ Please tick here if you would be willing to participate in further customer surveys.

☐ Please tick here if you would like to receive information on new titles or special offers from Thomas Cook Publishing (please note we never give your details to third party companies).

Please detach this page and send it to: **The Editor, Travellers, Thomas Cook Publishing, PO Box 227, The Thomas Cook Business Park, Peterborough PE3 8XX, United Kingdom.**

tear along the perforation

Publishing

The Editor, Travellers
Thomas Cook Publishing
PO Box 227
The Thomas Cook Business Park
Peterborough, PE3 8XX
United Kingdom